FAMILY BIKING

The Parent's Guide to Safe Cycling

Robert and Christie Hurst

FALCONGUIDES

GUILFORD, CONNECTICUT
HELENA, MONTANA

FALCONGUIDES®

An imprint of Rowman & Littlefield
Falcon, FalconGuides, and Outfit Your Mind are registered trademarks of Rowman & Littlefield.

Distributed by NATIONAL BOOK NETWORK

British Library Cataloguing-in-Publication Information available

Library of Congress Cataloging-in-Publication Data

Hurst, Robert (Robert J.)
 Family biking : the parent's guide to safe cycling / Robert and Christie Hurst.
   pages cm
 Includes bibliographical references and index.
 ISBN 978-1-4930-0989-3 (pbk. : alk. paper) — ISBN 978-1-4930-1503-0 (e-book) 1.
Cycling for children. 2. Cycling—Safety measures. I. Hurst, Christie. II. Title.
 GV1057.2.H87 2015
 796.6083—dc23

                                                                    2015028080

♾™ The paper used in this publication meets the minimum requirements of American National Standard for Information Sciences—Permanence of Paper for Printed Library Materials, ANSI/NISO Z39.48-1992.

Contents

Introduction

What is family biking? The term could refer to a slow cruise on a neighborhood bike path, a serious commute, or a shopping trip. We know of one dad who carried his kid up and over Independence Pass on a cargo bike. That qualifies. But the critical ingredient is kids. If you're riding with your kid(s), whether they be on board your own bike or cruising next to you on theirs, you're family biking. And that's the purpose of this book: To give biking parents who want to ride with their kids information on the issues that concern them most. From pregnant biking to teaching children to ride safely, it's all in here.

That's not us on the cover. We kind of wish it were. We're not that hot.

And we rarely get out for a recreational ride the likes of which these fine-looking young people appear to be enjoying. Almost all of our riding with our daughter, Bea, is utilitarian transport. Not that we think riding her to the daycare isn't fun. It is most of the time. Certainly it's a lot more fun than trying to drive there, which is a level of Hell. Every time we try to make that drive, we shake our fists at the sky and scream, Why?! Whyyyy?

On our bikes the trip is much more interesting, and also it seems much easier. It's definitely as fast or faster than it is in a car. We're lucky to have one of the world's fanciest bike paths—almost like a highway for bikes—within a few blocks of our house, running almost the whole way there, slipping beneath all the streets and intersections. If that fantastic infrastructure weren't in place, our bike commute would have a very different feel. Most family bikers aren't so lucky.

We're far from the most experienced family bikers out there. We readily admit to that. While we ride with her a lot, we only have one kid to haul around. There are moms and dads out there riding three kids—or more—every day, car-free. We can't hold a candle to them. They have figured out so much more than we have about the logistics and associated equipment of baby-hauling. About babies in general. But we've certainly been on our bikes much more than the average Jane and Joe. Between the two of us we have almost thirty years of bike messenger experience. Robert wrote several biking guides, and Christie pedals a 30-mile round-trip commute year-round, and kept it up through her pregnancy. We've paid our pedaling dues.

One way to do it: a city cruiser pulling a Weehoo trailer. *Courtesy Weehoo*

To fill in the gaps in our experience and to glean insights, we had conversations with as many family bikers as we could find, people with wide-ranging backgrounds. Even if you think you know everything, how will you know for sure unless you listen to others? We glommed on shamelessly to others' knowledge. Big thanks especially to Clarise Jenkins, Jonathan Maus, Alexis Rohde, Patrick Barber, Sally Ruiz, Kathy Steinhauer, Paul Stuckey, Rita Geller, Danielle Givens, and Kathy Gillis, whose contributions were not only crucial but cool.

One of the themes we came away with while compiling the info here is that every one of the available methods of family biking—front seat, rear seat, trailer, *bakfiets* (you'll learn some Dutch and Danish in this book), cargo trike, long-tail, tandem, or trailer bike—has its own certain coolness about it. We think some work better than others, but each has unique advantages. Each is particularly useful in its own way, and none is perfect.

The resulting book has three parts. **Part One** starts in the womb, with Christie's look at biking while pregnant. It then tackles some of the snarliest questions in family biking, like how young is too young to put a kid on a bike? What's the best way to carry an infant, if any? How should parents ride when carrying their kids? Is excessive vibration going to scramble your kid's brain? **Part Two** is the buyer's guide for family biking products, discussing everything from youth helmets to kids' first pedal bicycles. **Part Three** concerns itself with the issues that arise when the child is old enough to go pedaling off on her own.

Family biking is not without controversies, and this book does not shy away from them. Readers will learn about several, starting with a close look at kids' helmets and helmet standards that will surprise and anger some readers. We reexamine the American bias against bike-mounted child seats: As it so often does, the conventional wisdom got it all wrong. We debate the alleged safety of trailers, question the physics of rear-loaded cargo bikes, and throw the entire concept of training wheels off the Golden Gate Bridge. Finally, we won't shy away from the scariest question of all: Is it safe for my child to ride on the streets? This is a question we'll struggle with in our own family before too long.

About the Buyer's Guide
We took many of the photos, but also requested stock photos from the manufacturers. We thank them for giving us permission to use their photos and apologize if they sent us something that didn't get used.

One of the smallest balance bikes available, the Kinderbike E-Series has a tiny steel frame and a choice of pneumatic tires on alloy rims or airless on plastic rims. *Courtesy Kinderbike*

In no case has any manufacturer or seller of any of these products given us any product, payment, discount, or deal. (With one exception: FirstBIKE sent us a balance bike after the book was written and being edited.) Our sole contact with these companies has been to request product photos and ask occasional questions. Some of the small builders were very generous in answering questions about their products and about the industry in general. We're very happy to showcase relatively tiny businesses that don't have big corporate connections or advertising budgets, and that don't cut corners on quality. Unfortunately their stuff is usually really expensive, so we don't get to actually own much of it.

Products mentioned are not necessarily intended to be endorsements of those products. Certainly, not all the products listed perform in a really stellar way in the field. We felt it was important to list products for a wide range of budgets, but it wasn't our intention to produce comprehensive lists of every family biking product available. Undoubtedly some cool products were left out, and maybe a few uncool products are included that should not have been. It was not our intention to disappoint or upset anybody in the industry, so if there are any ruffled feathers from perceived slights, omissions,

The benefits of family biking—beyond just getting from point A to point B—will last a lifetime. *Thinkstock*

or inaccuracies, we did not intend it. We'd like to see a whole lot more family biking and a whole lot more family biking products being purchased in this world.

Prices

Listing prices in a book is problematic because you know those prices are all going to be different before too long, probably before the book can be updated. But we thought it was important to list them in order to give potential buyers useful information for comparing the specifics of different products. In almost all cases we have listed the manufacturer's suggested retail price. Just be aware that the listed prices may have changed or that some products could be available for different prices from different outlets.

Part One:
PRECIOUS CARGO

CHAPTER 1

Biking for Two

An easy way to get started biking with your baby is to ride with the little nipper safely tucked away in your uterus. No special equipment to buy, no trailers to hook up, no reviews of baby helmets to read. Just you, your bike, and that tiny human you're cooking up inside you. Especially if you biked regularly before becoming pregnant, you can usually continue to do so safely throughout your pregnancy. Some of pregnancy's most gruesome discomforts—like nonstop morning sickness, charley horses, and gripping anxiety—can be alleviated somewhat through cycling. Of course, the question of whether to ride during pregnancy is deeply personal, and the answer will probably be different for every woman and every pregnancy.

The general pregnancy advice from that sedentary woman at work, your worried mother-in-law, and your best friend might be the type of fear-mongering that makes you afraid to leave the house, let alone hop on your bike and cruise.

Don't eat lunchmeat! Are you really going to eat that goat cheese? Don't you know that you should keep your laptop away from your belly? Seat belts are dangerous! Don't lift your arms above your head or the umbilical cord will strangle the baby!

Sometimes it can seem as though pregnant women should be sitting very still on little pillows, taking only small breaks to eat enormous amounts of food. All that well-meant advice can make pregnancy a scary time.

Biking during pregnancy is good for fetal development. *Fuse/Thinkstock*

As ridiculous as some of the recommendations seem (our arms really aren't connected to the umbilical cord, just in case you were wondering), it can be hard not to let it reverberate a little. You start to wonder . . . *What if this slice of turkey gives me listeria? What if something bad happens to the baby after I drink this cup of coffee?* It's not much of a stretch from there to *What if I overheat while biking?* or *What if I fall off my bike?* or, even worse, *What if I get hit by a car?* These fears, especially the ones about getting injured, are valid.

That anxiety can compound into a full-on existential crisis when mixed with uncertainties about how your life will change due to pregnancy and the resulting baby. Fears that you might lose your previous hobbies or passions are common and real. Mix all those worries together into one cranium stew pot, and it's enough to drive you bonkers.

Exercise during Pregnancy

Fortunately for those who want to maintain their fulfilling, active lifestyles during pregnancy, research tells us that exercise is beneficial for both pregnant women and their babies. Way back in 2002 the American Congress of Obstetricians and Gynecologists (ACOG) announced that pregnant women could safely exercise at a moderate intensity for at least 30 minutes a day, as long as there were no complications in the pregnancy. Not only could pregnant women exercise safely, but that exercise was good because it might prevent gestational diabetes.[1]

The ACOG cautioned about some situations when pregnant women should not exercise; conditions such as severe anemia, poorly controlled seizure disorders, and extreme morbid obesity were a few of the items on the list. Aside from the recommendation that pregnant women exercise, the most important idea in their findings is that pregnant women should definitely consult a doctor to make sure it is okay to exercise. So before you lube your chain and don your spandex, please see your doctor.

While the recommendations about whether to exercise are pretty cut and dried, advice on exertion levels is less so. Some doctors still advise women not to get their heart rates above 140 beats per minute, which is outdated advice. In 1985 the ACOG published the magical 140 number as a maximum heart rate for pregnant exercising women.[2] But in 2003 they reneged, which was good, because 140 beats per minute for a sedentary woman might be soul-crushing exercise, while for a very fit woman it could feel like walking the dog.

Borg Rating of Perceived Exertion

6		Doesn't count as exercise.
7	Very, very light	Like watching Netflix.
8		
9	Very light	
10		Doesn't really count as exercise.
11	Fairly light	Like casually strolling with the dog.
12		Target range for exercise during pregnancy.
13	Somewhat hard	You should be able to chat, but not sing.
14		
15	Hard	
16		Whoa, back it off, sister! This might be
17	Very hard	too hard to sustain if you're pregnant!
18		But talk to your doctor to make sure.
19	Very, very hard	
20	Vomiting on a mountain	

Instead of using a target heart rate, the ACOG advised that women use a perceived rate of exertion scale. The Borg Rating of Perceived Exertion (above) is a nifty way to figure out how hard you are exercising. The scale, which goes from 6 to 20 (one wonders why it doesn't just start at 1), measures activity level from resting to maximal exertion by asking you to honestly rate yourself on how hard you feel you are working.[3] So, 6 is like sitting on the sofa binge-watching reality TV; 20 is puking at the top of a 13,000-foot mountain during a grueling race. The ACOG recommends that most pregnant women exercise somewhere between 12 and 14 (moderate exertion).[4] A woman who begins pregnancy in peak fitness will probably go farther and faster at a 13 than a woman who is a very casual exerciser.

The Health Benefits of Exercising While Pregnant

In their 2002 recommendations the ACOG decided that exercising during pregnancy might prevent gestational diabetes.[5] That is a good thing, but is just the beginning of the benefits we get from exercise. One study showed that exercise might stave off depression in pregnancy, that active women who engaged in moderate to vigorous physical activity were about half as likely to have "high depressive symptoms" as women who didn't.[6]

Another study found that exercise in the first two trimesters of pregnancy might be associated with a lower rate of cesarean sections.[7] Some studies even say that exercise during pregnancy increases fetal growth, possibly because of improved blood flow in the placenta.[8] Even better, a 2012 study done by researchers at the University of Montreal determined that exercise during pregnancy has a positive effect on newborns' cognition.[9]

As if all that weren't enough to persuade you to exercise while being a human incubator, probably the best reason is that for short periods of time, exercise can allow you to pretend that your life isn't about to drastically change in many frightening ways. While you're sweating and breathing, you can have a respite from worrying about things like your changing identity, the shift in your relationship, or inadvertently poking the newborn's soft spot. If you were active before becoming pregnant, exercise can keep you grounded and give you something from your pre-baby life to hold on to. If you are new to exercising, it can help forge a new piece of yourself that is somewhat apart from the baby.

When to Slow Down or Stop

The ACOG means it when they say to check with your doctor before exercising while pregnant. Your doctor will know all the contraindications and will also be able to judge from your medical and athletic history what sort of personal recommendations to offer. If you get the go-ahead, the ACOG has published a list of warning signs that you should stop exercising. Some are obvious, like vaginal bleeding, preterm labor, decreased fetal movement. Others are more vague: Headaches, dizziness, or calf pain might not seem like immediate warning signs, but they are.

Provided you have no complications, you should be able to exercise through the duration of your pregnancy. Many women find that they slow down as the baby grows and have to reduce the duration or frequency of exercise. Some types of exercise can become too uncomfortable. Listen to your body; talk to your doctor.

This slowing down during pregnancy can be hard, especially if it's unexpected. Some women who are used to competing may feel frustrated when fatigue, morning sickness, or shortness of breath interferes with activities, which might even seem like a downside to exercising. Mother of two Alexis

Rohde said, "The only drawback [to exercising while pregnant] was a bit of a frustration over what I felt to be a loss of fitness and shortness of breath. I definitely felt like I had some decreased lung capacity, especially toward the end. That impacted my endurance and I felt winded. Maybe if I had some better information on what to expect, it wouldn't have felt so frustrating?"[10] So, to all you pregnant, exercising women, consider this your heads up. You will slow down.

The Risk of Falling

When the ACOG published its guidelines in 2003, they did not fully rule out any activities for pregnant women. However, they did identify scuba diving and exercises performed while in a supine (lying down on your back) position as risks during pregnancy. They also identified sports that increase the risk of falls (skiing) and joint stress (jogging), and suggested extra caution for pregnant women participating in these sports.[11] Many doctors advise their patients not to participate in sports that pose a risk of abdominal trauma, such as hockey, basketball, and skydiving. Cycling is not mentioned on the list. Stationary cycling is even mentioned as "useful."[12]

In general, factual evidence about the risk of crashing while pregnant is almost nonexistent, which isn't too surprising. Unfortunately that means that there is no specific statistical data to help you decide whether to ride while pregnant.

The perceived risk of falling off your bike while pregnant might be enough to sway you against riding, or to convince you to ride a stationary bike, or to pursue other activities altogether. That makes sense. When pregnant women fall, there's the risk of placental abruption, preterm labor, or other problems that may pose a serious risk to the mother or baby.[13]

For many women it makes sense to continue riding. An experienced cyclist who sticks with riding as her pregnancy progresses might feel confident and safe on the bike, especially at first. Of course, her balance will change as her belly grows. Some doctors warn women to stop riding entirely due to balance issues; others encourage women to continue but to be careful. The weight gain and body changes usually happen slowly. If you continue to ride throughout your pregnancy, you might end up naturally compensating for changes and not notice a huge difference in your balance.

Just because you continue to ride doesn't mean you will ride the same as you did before. Most pregnant bicyclists take basic precautions that make the risk much lower: riding slower, turning conservatively to prevent slide-outs, and not riding on ice or in low-light situations.

Listen to your body and talk to your doctor to judge whether you want to continue riding. The upside is that it is low-impact exercise and easy on the joints (and your growing breasts!). It can also be more comfortable than other forms of exercise—if you are positioned correctly, it might take pressure off your back and/or belly.

Cycling Indoors

If you decide that cycling during pregnancy is okay, your first consideration will be minimizing risks and staying safe. The easiest option is to stick to indoor cycling options, like riding a trainer. The benefit of a trainer is that you can read books or watch *Buffy the Vampire Slayer* while riding. These are things that will be exponentially harder to do when the baby arrives. The downside of a trainer is that it doesn't get you out of your house into the fresh air and sunlight. It can feel monotonous and uninspiring.

Spin classes are another great option for pregnant women. The stable bikes can be adjusted to accommodate your changing body. Attending a class can also offer the camaraderie of your fellow spinners, along with the whip-cracking structure of your teacher. You are out of your house. Alexis attended spin classes throughout one of her pregnancies: "Spin class was nice for several reasons. It was nice that the gym had childcare for the older child. There was a bathroom close by that could be used at any time. It was climate controlled, so weather was never an issue. It was easy to refill your water bottle. . . . Also, it is very easy to tailor the class to your fitness goals: meaning, you can lower the intensity and not get stuck on the road for more time than you were planning to be gone."[14]

Choosing to cycle inside during pregnancy can come with dangers other than boredom: dehydration and overheating. Riding inside tends to make people feel hotter and sweatier than riding outside. If you decide to ride indoors, drink plenty of water, and, when possible, position yourself near a fan. Talk to your doctor about hydration requirements during pregnancy and the risks of overheating.

Pregnancy and the Bike

There is something about riding a bike outside that spin class or a stationary bike can't replicate. Maybe it's the lure of the open road. Maybe your bike is your primary mode of transportation, in which case continuing to bike may be a necessity. In any event, if you are an experienced cyclist who feels confident about continuing to ride on the road, the first issue to contemplate is equipment.

During your first trimester, you can probably ride the same bike. In fact, riding the same bike at least for a while will probably be easiest because you are used to the geometry and the handling.

If you ride a road bike, it might get a little harder to maintain your position or to stay on the same bike as the baby grows. You might need to raise your handlebars and sit up more as time goes on. At some point you might feel more comfortable switching to a hybrid-style bike or a mountain bike, because they can offer more stability. If you change bikes, be mindful of your balance. A different bike will handle differently. It's a good idea to start with short rides along safer routes, so you get used to how the bike turns and stops.

Some women actually prefer the less upright position of a road bike throughout their entire pregnancies. Leaning forward can seem to take the pressure of your basketball-size belly off your organs and your back. It might seem to detangle the baby from your ribs and allow you to breathe almost freely. If you continue to ride a road bike, you might find that in your third trimester you need to pedal with your knees pointed out a bit so that your legs don't brush your belly. If you do, monitor yourself closely for knee pain. Knees are sensitive to micro adjustments, and possibly even more so when the relaxin hormone (which limbers up your body to prepare it for birth) is coursing through your body. While relaxin does a great job of loosening your pelvic girdle for birth, it also makes pregnant women more susceptible to injuries.[15]

Most important, listen to your body—if your balance is compromised, change your position or your bike. Make sure you feel comfortable and stable. Trust your instincts, talk to your doctor, and stay safe.

Bike Accessories

Maybe you are happy, comfortable, and stable on your bike. Excellent! To keep it that way, a couple of extra considerations that can affect your safety need attention. First, your brakes: Check them regularly, and make sure they work. If they are out of adjustment, fix them. Also ensure that your shifting happens smoothly, and that your chain is not about to snap like a dried twig. Terrible bike wrecks can happen when bikes aren't shifting well or when chains unexpectedly break or skip. Check your wheels for problems, and make sure your tires aren't wearing through (blowouts can cause wrecks). Basically, give your bike a safety inspection. Wrecks due to mechanical problems are bad. Those wrecks while pregnant are much worse.

Pedals are another issue. If you use clipless pedals, check them for problems. For any type of pedal, make sure all the threaded parts are screwed together properly and won't come loose. Certain types of clipless pedals can break right on the mechanism that keeps your feet clipped in. This can be dangerous while pedaling and even more so when coming to a stop—we've all seen at least one cyclist in clipless pedals topple over at a stoplight. Some women might feel comfortable switching from clipless to flat pedals to avoid problems altogether.

The bike seat can be another problem—not necessarily for safety but for comfort. Bike seats are notoriously uncomfortable. Many cyclists search for years to find one they like and, when they do, they buy them in bulk in case their favorite model is ever discontinued. Unfortunately, as your mini-me grows, so will your pelvis. This could turn your favorite bike seat into a medieval torture device. Women-specific seats are often a little wider and might offer some comfort.

Route and Riding Style

Once you are comfortable and solid on your bike, the next consideration is your route. Most experienced cyclists are probably attuned to the importance of route selection, but the issue is even more important when you're riding for two. Besides, figuring this out pre-baby will help in the long run if you decide to ride with the little whippersnapper post-birth.

If you are a bicycle commuter, are there any dicey sections of the route you should change? If you have a favorite road ride, are there any sketchy intersections? Reroute yourself accordingly. You might consider riding on a bike path or along a marked bike route. It could take longer to get where you're going, but that is a good tradeoff for safety. Keep in mind that bike paths are not immune from crashes. Minor crashes might even be as likely or more likely to occur on bike paths than on streets.

If you are used to riding on rough sections of road, it will help to find a smoother street. Keep your eyes peeled for potholes or unexpected road damage. Riding on a well-lit road (if you are riding before dawn or after dark) is important. If you don't have them already, invest in a good set of lights, front and rear, and use them in any low-sunlight situation. Use a lot of reflectors and reflective tape.

Even if you feel that your route is safe, you will probably find that as your pregnancy progresses, your riding style changes. You might become purposefully slower and even more vigilant than usual. You might stop bunny hopping, going off curbs, zooming around corners, or generally doing anything that could increase the risk of a fall. Let your common sense guide you, and change your riding style to become as cautious as possible.

Maternity Bike Clothes

Bike clothing probably won't be an issue for much of your pregnancy, if at all. Some women manage through pregnancy in all of their regular bike ensembles. If you are a bike commuter who typically rides while wearing civilian clothes, you can simply carry on riding in your maternity wardrobe. But if you are a commuter with a long ride or a recreational rider or competitive cyclist, and your usual biking wardrobe stops working for you, you have to problem-solve or invest in some new pieces.

The wonderful thing about bike clothes is that they are typically stretchy and forgiving, especially during that early phase of pregnancy when you're just puffy and somewhat chesty, like you've been hitting the Bloody Marys a little too hard. But sometime in the second trimester, it might get more difficult to make your jersey meet your shorts. In this case you could designate one or two regular maternity shirts as your riding gear; in cooler weather you could layer a maternity shirt under your jersey.

Your regular bike shorts might fit the bill throughout your pregnancy. But if not, maybe you have an old, stretched-out pair in the bottom of a drawer. If you haven't gotten rid of them, they might work for your maternity riding outfit. If that doesn't work, some crafty women find that they can sew a stretchy panel into the front of their biking shorts to make them work for the later months of pregnancy.

It can be more difficult to find a jacket that covers you and baby, but not impossible. Borrowing a larger jacket from a friend might work, or just try a new one in a larger size. If regular bike clothes aren't working and you don't want to size up or borrow from a friend, you have options. A quick Internet search reveals lots of maternity exercise clothes, although fewer cycling-specific selections. If you need to, let maternity athletic gear do double duty. Use those maternity yoga leggings for biking. Wear a regular maternity workout shirt for biking, because really, there is no rule that says cyclists have to wear cycling clothes.

One wardrobe item that you probably can't borrow and will have to buy is a good athletic bra. Breasts change size significantly throughout pregnancy, and many women experience considerable breast pain and tenderness. A comfortable, supportive bra is a must. As your body changes, you might have to invest in a few different ones throughout your pregnancy.

Bike shoes could be a more expensive issue. Some women find that their feet get larger in pregnancy. If you have a pricey, fancy pair of bike shoes, you might find that they no longer fit and you need new ones. Or you might have safety issues with your bike shoes. Teetering around on slick-soled shoes with metal nubs on them can be a disaster, even when you are not pregnant. If you do not feel safe in your shoes, switching from a slippery road shoe to a rugged mountain bike shoe might be safer. Skipping bike shoes entirely is also an option.

Postpartum Cycling

Once the little bundle of joy has made an appearance, you can get back to your old routines as soon as your health care provider gives you the go-ahead and as soon as you feel ready. Many factors come into play. If you had a cesarean section, an episiotomy, or significant tearing, for instance, the road back will be longer. There are emotional factors, such as whether you want to be away from the baby. Some are also practical—you need to provide childcare, and, of course, if you are nursing you have to time everything just so. Or, if you bike for transportation, you might have to get back to the bike as soon as possible.

One of the hardest factors might be the emotional one. On one hand, you just want to snuggle with the baby. On the other hand, you are so tired of just snuggling the baby. You might be exhausted and a little off-kilter. You might feel judged for wanting to take time away from the baby.

Danielle Givens, another biking mom, "started bike commuting the day I went back to work after leave (twelve weeks postpartum), and it was a fantastic way to get the weight off and get back into shape. Also, with limited time to work out, it combined my commute and workout in one so I didn't lose any time with the baby."[16]

Getting back into an exercise routine or back to riding for transportation after pregnancy can help to normalize the wild change your life has just taken. It is also good for you. Many studies show that postpartum exercise improves quality of life, reduces risks of certain diseases,[17] and can lessen the effects of mild to moderate postpartum depression.[18]

When you return to the bike, be sure to ease back into it. Just like when you were pregnant, listen to your body, and to your doctor. In some ways it might be easier than when you were pregnant—you won't be toting around a big belly anymore. But there might still be challenges. This was true for Alexis. "I actually found nursing and exercise more of a pain than exercising while pregnant," she said. It was difficult to time her exercise schedule around her nursing schedule. And then there was the issue of breast pain. "I found I did lower-impact stuff for a while."[19] Biking and spin classes fit the bill here, but remember, if you are nursing, wear a good bra.

CHAPTER 2

Infants on Bikes: How Young Is Too Young?

New parents who hope to begin transporting their babies on bikes are going to run into a brick wall placed there by various American Powers That Be, who have determined that one is the magic number. One year old. After that, go for it. Before that, no way. For instance, this is the declaration handed down from the American Academy of Pediatrics, an organization that provides weighty recommendations to physicians, recommendations that are taken very seriously.

Lately much of the concern about infants on bicycles revolves around the question of excessive vibration, but the AAP has never mentioned vibration as an issue. Originally the AAP's recommendation stemmed from the typical baby's alleged inability to hold her little head up with a helmet on it. Their necks aren't strong enough to hold up helmets, they said, so no riding. No matter how strong your baby's neck might be, if you want to put a helmet on the kid, or are compelled to by law, you're going to have a tough time finding one that will fit your child's little head until she's closing in on a year old anyway. They don't make helmets for smaller babies. So the AAP's old one-year restriction, dating to the 1990s when the helmet regulations were being finalized, comes very much as an attachment to the helmet biz.

The one-year rule is also enshrined, indirectly, in some state laws. Twenty states so far and countless localities have laws requiring kids to wear

Commonplace in Europe, but controversial in the United States: This method of traveling with an infant—with a car seat strapped into a cargo box or trailer—could be illegal depending on the laws where you live. *Courtesy Babboe* helmets while pedaling or riding on bikes. Parents who live in these places are forced to wait until their children can wear and support helmets, unless they want to ignore the law. New York State and Massachusetts took it one giant step beyond, making it illegal to bike with a child under 1 year, helmet or no helmet.

So the barriers to biking with younger babies go far beyond intense cultural pressures. They're institutionalized far and wide.

The American Academy of Pediatrics' one-year rule can be blasted for a few different reasons. First, the AAP completely ignores the possibility of carrying a baby in an infant carrier or car seat that is strapped into a trailer or the wooden box of a cargo bike. This is a widely used method in the world of family biking. When a baby is carried on a bicycle this way, a helmet should not be used. Many pediatricians warn parents not to try to put a helmet on an infant who is strapped into a car seat or carrier, because the helmet could force the infant's head down and affect the airway, making it difficult for the child to get enough oxygen. Car seats aren't meant to be used with helmets. They are already designed to protect the occupant's head in case of a crash, with high sides and a sort of roll bar. (Interestingly, Georgia passed a law requiring children under 1 year to not only wear helmets but be carried in infant carriers in trailers, or in slings—their state legislature thus requiring something that is considered dangerous for babies.)

Second, even if you agree to wait until the child can wear a helmet, all kids are different. This is hardly a revolutionary idea, but the AAP seems to have disregarded it, momentarily, when they made this recommendation. Kids develop at wildly different rates and in different ways. Some are unusually strong and muscular at a young age. Some have heads big enough for American helmets when they are 9 months old or younger. Others may not be ready months after their first birthday. Age guidelines are often less than useful. In this case the recommendation could cheat many parents and children out of precious months of riding together; it could lead other parents to put helmets on 1-year-olds who aren't yet ready.

There has been quite a backlash brewing against the arbitrary one-year rule, based on the testimony of experienced baby-hauling parents. Many parents have transported their young babies by bike, despite the warnings and institutionalized barriers, and are talking about their experiences in social forums, blogs, and the like. We've heard of several weeks-old babies carried on bikes (in car seats strapped into trailers or *bakfietsen*) and countless 6-month-old kids on bikes or in trailers. Overwhelmingly the messages have been positive and reassuring. Their experiences have been fun and unspectacular, with no apparent ill effects for the babies. At the same time, there is no danger chorus recounting the rides gone bad, the crashes, the unforeseen consequences of excessive vibration (more on that below). No apparent regrets.

"This is classic American safety-culture BS in my opinion," says Portland's Jonathan Maus of the AAP's stance. Maus is the founder and editor of a popular blog, BikePortland.org, and a father of three. "How many leaders within the AAP actually bike with their kids and/or bike regularly themselves? I doubt many do, so they take the same perspective on bicycling that most of America has: That it's generally unsafe. Not a big surprise. . . . I think parents should be able to choose for themselves. Our family and friends have taken infants as young as 3 months in trailers on long, overnight bike-camping adventures. Years later, all the kids are healthy and thriving."[1]

In addition to a growing body of anecdotal evidence from parents in the United States, we have much more of the same from parents in Europe, where biking with small babies is common and accepted. There is no apparent outbreak of childhood injury or damage corresponding to this prominent aspect of their culture. In fact, the countries in Europe with the most robust family biking cultures have the best child well-being on the continent and score far (*far*) better than the United States in that category.[2]

So with each day there is more evidence stacked against the AAP's recommendation.

In states and locales without child helmet laws, parents are legally okay to carry babies of any age on bikes. We won't give a blanket endorsement for doing so but agree that some kids will be ready to ride as passengers well before their first birthdays, with the proper precautions. It seems indisputable that some kids will be ready before others. It seems smart to evaluate the readiness of small children on an individual basis. Given the lack of real evidence supporting the AAP's one-year rule, and the existence of a car seat method that the AAP never considered, it really is a matter for you and your pediatrician.

Bea went for her first ride at about 10 months, sitting in the trailer without a car seat or infant carrier. Frankly, the only reason we didn't ride with her earlier is because we hadn't really heard anything about the possibility of using the car seat or special sling in the trailer. Like the AAP, we were ignorant. We only had a vague notion of what could be done, stacked against the vague and fearful notions of danger. And fear likes to win.

Riding with Infants

Riding with infants younger than 1 year old is, again, not recommended by
the American Academy of Pediatrics. But many parents do it, in the United
States and elsewhere. If you want to, or need to, follow these guidelines:

- Secure your infant in the harness of a car seat or infant carrier,
  which is strapped or latched securely into a trailer or *bakfiets*
  cargo bike. (See the "Front-Loading Cargo Bikes" chapter.) It
  is crucial that the carrier be secured in the trailer or box, that is,
  attached to it. If the carrier tumbles out of the box during a crash,
  the baby could be worse off than if she had not been placed in a
  carrier at all.[3]

- Take whatever measures you reasonably can to dampen vibration
  reaching the child. For instance, you can use equipment with built-
  in suspension, or try something crude like putting a folded up
  blanket under the carrier. Or both.

- Ride even more slowly than you would with an older child, to
  minimize vibration and jostling of the baby, and to minimize the
  chance of crashes.

- Do not put a helmet on an infant in a child seat or carrier. The helmet might force the child's head down and narrow his airway. Also, the smallest helmets are too large for almost all infants' heads, and the seat or carrier is designed to protect the head already. You might feel that kids without helmets shouldn't be on bikes under any circumstances. In that case, wait until your child is strong enough and big enough to wear a helmet—don't put a helmet on a baby in a car seat.

- Do not put an infant in a bike-mounted toddler seat, front or back; do not put an infant in an infant carrier mounted on the front or back of a "normal" bike.

- Make sure the infant is shaded from the sun.

- If your infant is unhappy or seems uncomfortable during the ride, she probably has a good reason. Infants are the world's greatest truth tellers. Listen to your baby! (Toddlers are another story.)

CHAPTER 3

The Hazards of Family Biking

Excessive Vibration

The timing was interesting to say the least. About the time it started to become clear that infants were being transported safely by bike in trailers and cargo boxes—helmetless in car seats—a new concern emerged: excessive vibration.

Nobody denies that infants are particularly vulnerable to extreme conditions. With their relatively giant heads and weak neck muscles, infants are more vulnerable to whiplash injuries than older kids and adults, should a crash occur. Their undeveloped spines could be damaged if forced to sit up in an unnatural position for too long. Their brains are much softer and more gelatinous than older kids' brains, the axons of their nerve cells yet unprotected (by a substance called myelin, which develops throughout childhood), and so those brains are relatively vulnerable. This is all well known.

Unfortunately, nobody knows just how much vibration those little brains can take, what should be considered dangerous, or how much vibration they actually receive during bike rides, trips in the car, or many other normal everyday activities. This is an issue that is just recently being examined in a serious way.

Bea and her dad are ready to see the sights in Barcelona, using an old-fashioned child seat on a Dutch bike. *Christie Hurst*

We already know that excessive vibration can be a big problem for adults. Operators of heavy machinery who sit all day in badly vibrating machines receive those vibrations throughout their bodies and suffer from a litany of nasty ailments as a result—back pain, impaired vision and balance, reproductive damage, circulation disorders, and digestive problems, to name a few. Lower back pain has the strongest association with vibration exposure.[1]

It's not difficult to imagine that vibration and jostling could be relatively dangerous to infants. Dr. Tord Alden imagined just that in 2009, when he explained his misgivings about bicycling with babies in an article on the aforementioned BikePortland blog: "It's not about crashes at all, it's about the potential for repeated mild trauma to the brain because of bumps associated with everyday road conditions. What is undocumented is what is happening to the brain during the bumps." Of course all imaginings are not created equal. Dr. Alden is a highly experienced pediatric neurosurgeon, and his guesses are probably more likely to be right than ours. "Neurodevelopment is critical during the younger years. An infant's brain is a bunch of neurons, uninsulated wires, if you will. During the first year the infant is developing the myelin sheath, which insulates the neurons and sets the stage for all the development and learning that the brain does next. If you had to pick a time when it is most important to protect the brain from excess vibration or bumps and jostling about, it would be during that first year after birth."[2]

Is the kid really receiving "repeated mild trauma to the brain" in a bike trailer? Or is that really a big exaggeration? The truth is we don't know.

The myelination process to which Dr. Alden alludes is ultra-important. Children develop fatty myelin casings around their neurons, like insulation around electrical wires, in a process that continues from infancy through adolescence. Without the well-developed myelin covering, the neurons won't work efficiently.[3] More specifically, abnormal myelin development could lead to disorders like autism, schizophrenia, and Attention Deficit Disorder (ADD). The critical importance of myelin to brain function is underscored by the existence of diseases like multiple sclerosis that are associated with myelin degeneration.[4]

But is it true that carrying an infant on a bicycle could negatively affect the myelination process? Undocumented. And if so, wouldn't the vibrations in cars be potentially dangerous as well? One of the few things we know about vibration in baby hauling is that kids in cars—in car seats—receive much more vibration than the driver of the car.[5] Nobody ever warns parents about that. And since myelination continues through the adolescent years, why should the warnings against excessive vibration be directed at infants only? So many questions.

Interestingly, the American Academy of Pediatrics, though mightily concerned about children wearing helmets, doesn't have much if anything to say about the danger of vibration when a baby is transported by bike or any other means. Vibration isn't mentioned in any of their bike-related recommendations.[6] We'll be watching to see if they pick up that ball and run with it.

This lack of solid information leaves parents to their own impressions and instincts.

Reducing Vibration

It's often good to step back for a second and look at the big picture. Let's remember that parents often *purposely* subject their babies to vibrations, because they know those vibrations have a calming effect on the infant. Car rides and vibrating infant carriers are crucial weapons in the parent's war on fussiness. If vibration were that dangerous to the myelin sheath, we'd all be in big trouble.

We agree that extreme vibrations can probably be harmful to children, and that riding as a passenger on a bike could potentially be harmful for that reason alone. Such harmful vibrations, however, do not seem to occur on a bike or in a trailer, except in more extreme circumstances. Rolling on a typical asphalt surface, though much rougher than a smooth concrete path, is unlikely to produce vibrations harmful to a passenger. Only when the surface is particularly rough do the nasty vibrations occur. We cross a section like this on our ride to school in the morning, a 50-foot-long ramp that has a rumble-strip-like surface built in for traction purposes. When we turn and look at Bea while we are rumbling down it, we can see the vibration on her face. We have to slow *waaaay* down, almost to walking pace, to keep her from getting rattled. Under normal circumstances, on normal surfaces, vibration levels experienced by the passenger are usually more akin to those that parents seek to apply to their infants for soothing purposes. Kids in trailers and bike seats often fall asleep peacefully as they would in the gently bouncing arms of a caretaker.

Unfortunately the budget of this book didn't allow for any truly scientific examination of vibration in baby hauling. At some point somebody needs to

Trailers can overturn for a few different reasons, so try to avoid placing heavy objects like pumpkins in the compartment with your kid. *Robert Hurst*

put an accelerometer in a bike trailer and see what's up. More precisely, an accelerometer on the head of a child-size dummy in a trailer, child seat, and cargo box.

All we can really do is encourage parents to keep this vibration issue well in mind whenever they're riding with their kids. It's not safe to ride while looking behind you frequently or for very long, but monitoring your child more closely than you otherwise would can give you a good idea of just how much shaking is going on back there. Try using a mirror or, if you're really into it, a camera pointed backward so you can record what's going on while keeping your eyes on the road ahead. Review the footage when you get home. If you're part of a couple, ride next to your partner as she rides with the kid in tow or on board, and watch the child's head. You might be very surprised, even alarmed, at what you see.

You should also be aware of and thinking about mitigating harsh vibrations when walking with your child in a stroller or wagon and, while we're at it, when driving. The obvious way to mitigate the danger of vibration is to avoid riding over rough surfaces and, if you can't avoid them, to slow down enough or even walk the bike so the child isn't absolutely hammered. That's not an option in a car on the highway.

Beyond slowing down and avoiding rough surfaces, the easiest way to reduce vibration for a little trailer passenger is to let some air out of the trailer's tires. You can let quite a bit of air out without having to worry about it becoming a problem for the bike-trailer system. We rode with relatively low air pressure in the trailer's tires when we pulled our daughter around. It does make pulling the trailer a little more difficult, but may be worth it.

Those with bike-attached seats might be tempted to let a bunch of air out of their bike's tires. This is a much more delicate matter than letting air out of trailer tires. It will help with the vibration but if you run tires too soft on a bike, you compromise control and risk pinch flats. Drop the pressure somewhat, but take care. Simply getting bigger tires, if they'll fit, will help with vibration and allow you to play around more with air pressure. Bike seat users should really concentrate on riding slowly and choosing routes and surfaces that minimize the bumps.

Equipment choices can have a big effect on vibration. Use knobby mountain bike tires on smooth pavement, for instance, and you'll feel some extra vibration just from the tires. Large-diameter wheels are better at absorbing vibrations than small wheels. Stiff aluminum bicycle frames will transmit more vibration than lightweight steel frames.

Some baby-hauling equipment is specifically designed to minimize vibration. Some of the more expensive trailers have built-in mechanical suspension. Many infant slings sold as trailer accessories are designed to provide extra suspension. The floating type of rear-mounted child seat, which attaches to the bike's frame (usually to the seat tube), does a fair job at reducing vibrations and softening big hits. Rack-mounted seats, on the other hand, are notoriously bad in the vibration department.

Choking Hazard

Bringing snacks along on family biking excursions is one way to keep your kid in the game. Not bringing snacks along on rides could get a parent in some pretty hot water. What other metaphors can we use to describe the magic of snacks? Snacks are really useful and important.

Think twice, however, about handing your kid big hunks of food while they're in the trailer or child seat on the back of the bike. Our kid has had some scary moments of near-choking on food when sitting perfectly still at the table. Any jostling while rolling on the bike can add a dangerous complication, probably making it more likely that the child will have some sort of "swallowing mishap."

What makes this scary with regard to trailers or rear seats is that the child's position is behind you and out of sight. Turning around to check on the kid is not necessarily easy, and certainly makes it more likely that you'll collide with something. When riding with your child, you want to minimize the turning around. Keeping your eyes forward is a critical part of safe, defensive riding. With the kid up front, though, you can just set a picnic basket up there and let him go at it like Yogi Bear. If anything happens, you'll notice it right away.

Don't worry about it too much, as there's no epidemic of choking-while-biking incidents to speak of. Nobody talks about it, but we thought it warranted a mention.

Sunburn

In limited amounts, sun exposure is good for you and your child. However, sunburns are dangerous, especially to children. It might seem hard to believe, but sunburns in babies and toddlers are linked to skin cancers later in life.

The best ways to avoid sunburn are obvious. Avoid the sun and dress your little munchkins in clothing and hats that block the sun. The visors of kids' helmets don't do a great job of shading faces, but they could be worse. Carry a hat along to use when the helmet's off.

Sunscreen is another obvious line of defense. Pediatricians caution against using a lot of sunscreen on little kids because sunscreen is a somewhat nasty, poisonous substance that affects kids' health in ways we still struggle to understand. Through the first few years of life, a child's skin is still developing and doesn't form the same type of effective barrier that your adult skin does.[7] Baby and toddler skin is particularly sensitive to solar radiation—any radiation—but its ability to keep toxins, like those found in sunscreen, from being absorbed into the system is also limited. So we have a Catch-22 here.

Federal government agencies tell us not to put any sunscreen on infants in their first 6 months.[8] But this recommendation seems somewhat arbitrary, as with the AAP's recommendation against putting a child on a bike before the first birthday. It's based on very limited knowledge of the vulnerability of young skin and the toxicity of sunscreen. There is no known milestone in the development of the infant's skin that occurs around the 6-month birthday that suddenly makes applying sunscreen okay. It's one of those CYA (cover your butt) numbers: They figure 6 months probably covers it. And since family biking isn't something they care to discuss, they can't think of any good reason why an infant younger than 6 months old would be out in the sun at all.

Our pediatrician was adamant about our using kids' sunscreen on our daughter instead of the normal stuff. Sunscreen for kids is less likely to contain fragrances, hormone-disruptors, and other problematic chemicals. But even kids' sunscreen can contain all kinds of weird ingredients that could be harmful. A study by the Environmental Working Group found that 37 percent of so-called kids' sunscreens contained oxybenzone, a chemical that is known to disrupt hormones in potentially dangerous ways. Several of the alleged kids' sunscreens they tested had literally nothing in their ingredient lists to distinguish them from the regular sunscreens sold by the same companies. "Sometimes the words 'children' or 'kids' are just marketing gimmicks," cautions the EWG.[9]

So what should parents be looking for when they purchase sunscreen for their kids? Find a mineral-based sunscreen that claims to block UVA as well as UVB rays for "broad spectrum" protection. Both types of radiation cause sunburn, long-term damage, and skin cancer. American sunscreen makers have a tough time blocking ultraviolet A rays under current federal ingredient restrictions. UVA radiation penetrates deeper than UVB and is now suspected to be as damaging. Mineral-based sunscreens are more likely to offer good UVA protection, and are also less likely to contain harmful chemicals. (They also make your child look ghostly white, which is fun.)

Some types of mineral sunscreen are more dangerous to children than others and should be avoided. Stay away from sunscreens that use nano particles, which are more easily absorbed into the child's system. If the ingredient list contains oxybenzone or 4-MBC, look elsewhere.

The labels on tubes of sunscreen haven't always told true stories, unfortunately. *Consumer Reports* found that Alba Botanica and Banana Boat Kids' sunscreen "failed the wavelength test," even though their labels claimed broad spectrum protection.[10] We have slathered both brands on our daughter, of course, suckers for pretty labels on sunscreen, energy bars, wine bottles, and everything else.

Don't get too excited by high SPF numbers either. SPF (Sun Protection Factor) refers to a sunscreen's ability to block UVB rays, and a high number may actually indicate a lack of protection from UVA rays. Recently the FDA has been looking side-eye at sunscreens and the SPF number, which supposedly indicates how many times longer a sunscreened-up person can stay in the sun before burning. As it turns out, there is a lot of terribly misleading marketing hype involved. Who knew! Buy a sunscreen with an SPF of 15 or 30 or maybe 45. Anything higher than 50 is starting to get ridiculous. "FDA does not have adequate data demonstrating that products with SPF values higher than 50 provide additional protection compared to products with SPF values of 50," the feds say.[11]

Don't use spray sunscreen if you can avoid it. Parents and nannies love sprays for the convenience—sometimes putting sunscreen on a child can be a minor ordeal—but we don't want kids inhaling those particles. For convenience of application, try a stick. Sunscreen sticks look like big tubes of lip balm, and many parents find them much easier to use.

Make sure your kid doesn't eat any sunscreen. It's nasty enough when *not* ingested; we don't even want to think about what happens when your kid eats it. For this reason we recommend staying away from sunscreen that smells like delicious orange smoothies and things like that. (It's available.) Many experts caution against applying sunscreen to the child's hands, because the hands go into the mouth. As a general rule, use sunscreen sparingly, applying just enough to do the job.

Motion Sickness

Motion sickness is confusion itself! A child gets motion sick when one motion-sensing system in her body feels motion at the same time that another system thinks her body is at a standstill. Such conflicting signals are often sent when one's eyes are focused on a book or screen, sensing no motion, at the same time that the inner ear feels the body hurtling along the road. The same basic principle applies to airsickness, seasickness, and, we can assume, bikesickness. Of course, dictionaries of the English language don't contain that last word. Not yet.

It is not known why these conflicting signals cause a feeling of nausea (Greek for seasickness). There are several competing theories. Many scientists believe the body's ultimate response to this sense of disorientation, vomiting, is meant to remove toxins that the body assumes is causing the sickness—the body thinks some poison has been ingested and is trying to get rid of it. More confusion.

Kids between 2 and 12 are more prone than other humans to motion sickness; infants younger than 18 months old don't seem to get motion sick at all, which is a nice bonus for them and their parents. It's a good thing infants are immune to motion sickness or they would be even angrier little buggers upon emerging from the womb!

As with many other things, individual children are affected by motion sickness in different ways. Our 2-year-old doesn't seem to have any big issues with it even though she reads books—looks at books—while rocking along in the trailer. As forty-something persons, just thinking about doing that makes us want to heave. Many other kids get sick every time they take a car ride or bike ride, and that's got to be a huge pain for everyone involved.

Bikesickness might be cured very easily, by taking books and whatnot away from the child and encouraging her to look up and out, so her optical system can get reoriented to what's going on. Some parents report good results by augmenting their child's diet, making sure that there is some food in the stomach during the ride, but not a big greasy meal. Sleep is a proven alleviator of motion sickness, and some parents encourage napping during rides for that reason. If you have the option, take a break and pull over in a safe spot like a park to give your nauseated kid a chance to recover.

Our experience with adult car sickness leads us to believe that some drivers have habits behind the wheel that are especially conducive to causing sickness among the car's passengers. In particular, the sudden, jerky application of brakes or accelerator will often put us over the edge into nausea.

Certain cars seem to amplify uneven driving while others seem to dampen it. This makes us think that the same thing is probably true when traveling by bike—certain riding styles and setups are more likely to sicken passengers than others. It's something to consider if your child is consistently suffering from motion sickness. Maybe the problem is you. Ack! Solving the problem could be a simple matter of changing the machine, or changing the way you ride or drive. Slow down, smooth it out, and minimize jerky motions. In driving as well as bicycling, when trying to control the machine and smooth things out, a little physical relaxation will help a great deal.

Bike trailers probably cause more motion sickness than other modes of family biking. Not only do a trailer's passengers get jostled up and down, they sway back and forth constantly. Trailer passengers may also experience a strong lurching sensation as the "driver" accelerates. If your kid gets sick in the trailer, try changing your riding style; if that doesn't work, try carrying the child in a bike seat or in the bucket of a cargo bike.

As a last resort, look into medication. Many products claim to relieve motion sickness in children. Some of these products are not safe for younger toddlers, so talk to your pediatrician first. If you're looking for a natural antiemetic, try ginger.[12]

Cold

Cold, and inadequate planning for it, is a classic ride killer. If your passengers become uncomfortably cold, it can be difficult to recover. They may become apoplectic and inconsolable until you can get them inside where it's warm. Of course, if you really botch the job, extreme cold can present a serious danger for your child.

The main thing to remember about biking with little ones in cold temperatures is that your experience of the cold will be vastly different than theirs. You will be pedaling and burning energy and creating heat that just might overwhelm the cold and even make you feel uncomfortably toasty (of course, this depends on how cold it is, what you're wearing, and how hard you're working). Meanwhile your kid is just sitting there, feeling every bit of the cold and none of that calorie-burning warmth.

Trailers are really nice for cold temps because the covers that most trailers are equipped with offer some degree of protection. Blankets can also be used to great effect in trailers, whereas you don't want to use a blanket on the back of a long-tail or a child seat—too much opportunity for the blanket to wander into the spokes or drivetrain.

A *bakfiets* or cargo trike with a proper rain cover is probably the ultimate cold-weather baby-hauler. Unfortunately these covers tend not to be included with a cargo bike and cost quite a bit on their own—about as much as a decent trailer. Without a rain cover you can keep your passengers a little warmer by seating them backward in the cargo bucket.

Boredom

Boredom will kill a ride as surely as extreme cold. And, as with cold, boredom will sneak up on you undetected if you're not careful. Parents who love to ride might forget that their experience out there is different than their kids'. Some parents could pedal all day and not get bored. Kids' enthusiasm for the ride usually lasts about a half hour or so at a time, maybe less. That's true even for those kids who really love being on the bike.

Before writing off your kid's whining as simple boredom, rule out any genuine physical discomfort that might be a cause. She might be feeling sick, cold, or hot.

Experienced family bikers tend to give similar advice on this. Keep the rides short, they say. Longer rides should be broken up into segments, maybe 20 minutes per segment. It helps a great deal if there is some exciting destination at the end of each segment—something for the kid to look forward to.

Snacks. Don't forget the snacks.

Crashes and Collisions

Okay, here we go. This is what parental pedalers worry about the most. And rightly so, we must say. The danger is real. But the danger should also be examined rationally.

Generally speaking the relative danger of your child being injured in a crash, either while riding in a trailer or a child seat, is low. So exhale a little bit. While it's not something to ignore, it seems to be a very manageable danger. Injuries to properly strapped-in bike passengers could be described as rare. We hear of crashes and mishaps but very few actual injuries. Anecdotally, riding with children seems to be at least as safe as driving with them.

Keep in mind that bicycle injuries, as a whole, are not rare at all. Injured bicyclists journey to hospital trauma centers about half a million times per year in the United States. And about half a million more seek nonemergency medical attention after crashes.[13] Many of the victims are young kids who wrecked on their own bikes and were hustled off to the ER by worried caregivers; almost none of the injured are identified as passengers on their parents' bikes. Obviously the lack of passenger injuries follows largely from the fact that relatively few people ride bikes while carrying kids. But if there were something particularly dangerous about doing so, these stats would probably be speaking to us in different ways. We'll take a closer look at some of the available numbers in the ensuing chapters.

Car-bike collisions are the scariest and most deadly wrecks, but regular ol' wipeouts are much more common and cause millions of minor injuries each year in this country.[14] Typical causes of solo crashes include slippery turns, unseen potholes and curbs, and more insidious things like longitudinal cracks. For more on reading surfaces and avoiding wipeouts, see *The Art of Cycling* (2nd ed., FalconGuides).

Depending on which family biking mode you're using—child seat or trailer, cargo bike, or tandem—wiping out might be very dangerous for the passenger or surprisingly not dangerous at all. We'll discuss the pitfalls and special requirements of each mode in their respective chapters later in the book. In short, trailers are pretty good in wipeouts; bike-mounted seats are worse but not nearly as bad as commonly believed; and some cargo bikes may be prone to minor wipeouts. Trikes, of course, don't do too much crashing.

Obviously family biking will be easiest and solo crashes less likely if the operator of the bike is a highly skilled and experienced bike handler. That isn't always the case, however. Many parents are just getting into it and are learning as they go along. Learning, unfortunately, seems intimately related to crashing. Considering the astronomical numbers of solo crashes that are caused by inexperienced riders, it is a big concern for us. Ideally these new riders will figure out the basics of bike handling on their own, before carrying their kids.

Car-bike crashes cause fewer injuries, but the injuries they cause tend to be much more serious. About 30,000 American bicyclists were admitted to hospitals (one step above ER visits) in 2013.[15] No way could we describe serious bicycling-related injuries as rare. When you start to dissect it, however, that number doesn't look quite so bad. Children and teens acting badly are responsible for many serious collisions, and late-night drunken bicyclists are responsible for another big chunk of them. When you finally get to the sober adults, the pile is quite a bit smaller. It's a double-edged sword for a parent. Parental riding is surprisingly safe, but child biking is disturbingly dangerous.

Sober, law-abiding adult bicyclists still get hit by cars. These crashes can be divided into two general columns. One contains the collisions that the riders can't do much about. Hits from behind, things like that. Kind of like getting hit by a meteorite. The other column contains wrecks that could be avoided through awareness and defensiveness on the part of the bicyclist. (See the "Defensive Biking for Parents" chapter.)

Excessive Fear

Add excessive fear to the list of hazards in family biking. You'll have to watch out for it and avoid it as you would rough sections of road or patches of ice.

In our opinion, the amount of energy spent by the American Pediatric Association and other groups in cautioning biking parents—haranguing them with the arbitrary one-year rule and repeating scary, evidence-free warnings about bike seats—is wildly disproportionate to the relative risks. Their priorities seem way off. But it isn't just semi-obsolete safety organizations that are slinging mud all over the idea of riding with kids. This is a societal issue.

Don't be surprised if some random individuals throw you some attitude when they see you riding with your child. Some people—blissfully unburdened by factual knowledge on the subject—already believe that bicycling is extremely dangerous and that those who do it are irresponsible daredevils, so the sight of a child in a seat or trailer or on their own little bike can put them right over the edge. (Meanwhile they're speeding through school zones in SUVs—but never mind that.)

Society's excessively fearful view of carrying kids on bikes is part of a larger phenomenon, in which some dangers that are in reality very small get pumped up to colossal proportions, while others that are very real and damaging on a wide scale are all but ignored. This disconnect has become so comically obvious that it has generated some backlash. Blatant hypocrisy often does, thankfully.

Not long after a mom was arrested in 2014 for letting her 9-year-old walk to the park by herself, Petula Dvorak wrote a piece for the *Washington*

Post decrying this cultural absurdity. She pointed to the mass blindness to the carnage of driving: "About 300 kids are hurt daily in car accidents; an average of three are killed that way every day. Yet I don't see police pulling parents over and locking them up whenever they see someone in a car seat. But playing on the monkey bars without Mommy nearby? Book 'em!"[16] We share her frustration.

It's more than just overblown safety-mongering behind the bike scare. Bicycles give freedom to individuals, which is a frightening prospect to parents and others. Bicycles *are* freedom. Bicycles, though much older than cars, also represent change, a new way of moving through cities, a new way of life. A lot of entrenched interests don't want that kind of change, so excessive fear serves them well.

CHAPTER 4

Defensive Biking for Parents

Drivers Overlook Bicycles

When it comes down to it, defensive bicycling is about taking responsibility for your own safety or, in this case, your child's safety. The rider who puts his safety in the hands of others and expects everything to turn out all right will end up disappointed and, probably, crunched.

This isn't some groundless bike messenger bluster. If you look at collision statistics, you'll see (if you can sort out the kids' crashes from the adults') that most of the adults who collide with cars are not legally at fault in their crashes. They were following the rules but got hit anyway after motorists failed to notice them. That's what traffic's all about right there.

The tendency of drivers to overlook bicyclists is the single most important thing to understand about riding on the streets. We hope you can grasp this concept without having to learn the hard way, like many bicyclists do.

Route Choice

Taking responsibility for yourself and your child in traffic begins with route choice. New bike commuters get burned by this all the time. Instead of taking advantage of the bike's versatility, they just embark on the same routes they drive each day. That's not necessarily a good plan.

With a kid on board, most parents are already going to step up their route-finding game and seek out what they feel are the safest, easiest routes. Much of the beauty of the bicycle as urban transport lies in its ability to go so many different places, crossing back and forth between the pedestrian and vehicular realms. However, freedom becomes a liability in the wrong hands.

Use all tools available, including streets, paths, and, when appropriate, sidewalks. Parent pedalers gravitate to the sidewalks, which may or may not be the best way to go. Sidewalk riding is an advanced course that requires more discussion (see "Sidewalk Riding" below).

Find routes with the least intensity of traffic possible. That is, choose routes that minimize high speeds and angry drivers, and avoid strip mall exits, high schools, and other seething pits of motorized madness. Don't ride next to parked vehicles, lest you be mercilessly doored. If you think you can spot people inside parked cars and predict when doors might open, you're wrong. Bike lanes often invite riders into the Door Zone, but riding on the left edge of the bike lane will usually keep you out of it.

Often a great cycling street can be found one block on either side of the most direct route, which is usually a heinous high-speed boulevard lined with fast-food joints and liquor stores. In such cases it's worth it to go a little bit out of the way.

Riding with a kid usually means foregoing some of the tricky shortcuts you used to enjoy when riding alone. You're not going to want to dart across some eight-lane boulevard or carry a kid-hauling bike, child not included, up any stairs. Some modes of family biking will have particular route restrictions.

Riding the Streets

You probably already know that you should ride according to the basic vehicular rules of the road. You should ride on the right half of the road, with traffic. Riding against traffic causes all kinds of extra danger and really raises the likelihood of a collision. You probably know you shouldn't run red lights and all that. But maybe you don't know much about safe riding beyond riding predictably, according to the rules. If that's the case, you've got a lot to learn.

Trailers like this low-end Burley are versatile tools for family transportation. They can haul cargo as well as kids and can be attached to just about any bike you already have. You can remove the trailer and get your old bike back at any time. However, many parents feel uneasy about pulling their kids on the street. *Robert Hurst*

How do you approach an intersection when the light is green? Your answer could reveal much about what kind of rider you really are.

If you're like most people, you just kind of daydream your way right through it. Any brainpower you bring to the endeavor is used up keeping yourself in the lane. Beyond that you're just assuming that everything will work out, and are probably thinking about something else entirely. The light is green after all, and green means go. By golly, most of the time you go sailing under those green lights without any trouble. Until one day . . .

When approaching a green light intersection, use the same mindset and technique you would use if the light were red and you were planning on running it (which of course you wouldn't, because you're a fine upstanding citizen). Keep your awareness on high. Begin early and search for potential encroachers, from all angles—from behind, from the right and left, from straight ahead. They may as well be dropping from the sky. You see, the green light doesn't really matter much. Drivers will be crossing through the intersection anyway, often at speed—making rights on red and turning left from the oncoming lanes. That's not to mention the possible light-runners, just blasting through from either side, and the jay-runners darting across. All players share one thing in common: a persistent inability to notice an approaching bicyclist and child.

The good news is that most every type of encroachment that you face while riding through intersections can be avoided, even when drivers completely fail to see you. But you have to be ready for them. You have to be one step ahead. Nobody else is going to take care of you and your child in traffic. Nobody but you.

Sidewalk Riding

With kids on board, or in the trailer, pedaling parents quite naturally spend more time riding on sidewalks than do other bicyclists. We gravitate toward spaces that seem safe from motor traffic. Unfortunately it is illegal almost everywhere in the United States for an adult to ride a bike on a sidewalk, whether hauling a toddler or not. There are exceptions to this. Seattle and Portland, for instance, the hotbeds of family biking in the United States, allow sidewalk riding under certain circumstances. Some cities allow sidewalk riding by adults outside the central business districts. But most family biking that occurs on sidewalks is actually illegal biking. The cops may not care enough to give you a ticket, the people you see might not mind or even notice, but that illegality suddenly has far-reaching implications when something goes wrong out there.

Legal or illegal, sidewalk cycling in general requires more awareness and finesse—more engagement—than riding on the street. It's tricky. Sidewalk riding has its own weird set of common occurrences and potential mishaps that is separate and distinct from the street's. Riders who move to the sidewalk to escape the obvious dangers of the street often overlook the hidden dangers of the sidewalk.

Sidewalk riding can also be inconsiderate if pedestrians are trying to use the same space. If peds are blocking the sidewalk, let them be. Don't charge around them or make them move. It's their world and you're just visiting. Giving pedestrians their due on sidewalks is prudent but can be a time-sapper. Still, such things can be overcome with a little bit of awareness and consideration.

Beware of blanket generalizations about sidewalk riding. The most common thing that bicyclists hear about sidewalks is how hazardous they are for two-wheeling. "Sidewalk riding is more dangerous than riding in the street!" squawks the Internet, never failing to seize the opportunity to mansplain at new riders with such a deliciously counterintuitive nugget of wisdom.

It's certainly possible to look at the available accident surveys in a way that "proves" the relative danger of sidewalk riding—the frequency of crashes is shown to be higher for sidewalk riders. But dig into the numbers a little bit and you will notice a few things. First, notice how a huge percentage of sidewalk-related crashes involve kids. Kids are known for riding on sidewalks and making bad mistakes that lead to crashes. Are you, an adult, going to make the same type of kid mistakes? Probably not (although keep this all in mind when the time comes to teach your kid to ride on her own). Second, notice that the crashes that are blamed on the sidewalk tend not to occur on the actual sidewalk. They occur where that sidewalk crosses driveways, alleys, and street intersections. In other words, this alleged danger inherent in sidewalks is still really about the streets. Bicyclists don't get hit by cars on sidewalks, but where sidewalks meet motorways. Understanding this crucial distinction is the beginning of sidewalk safety.

Your instinct tells you that riding on the sidewalk is safer for you and your child. Your instinct could very well be correct. Technically. Riding in spaces that are closed to motor traffic virtually eliminates the chance of being hit by a car. Unfortunately you might not be seeing the big picture. Your instinct might not realize that the sidewalk provides a very intermittent refuge, interrupted at frequent intervals by motorways. These motorways can be obvious, like an eight-lane boulevard that has to be crossed. Or these motorways might be hidden, interrupting the sidewalk sneakily. Your first job as a sidewalk biker, after ceding the space to the pedestrians who belong there, is recognizing these interruptions. Any time the sidewalk crosses a driveway or alley, no matter how minor, the sidewalk ceases to exist. It is canceled. At that moment you and your child are crossing into the motorized realm, and you should think and act accordingly.

Most obviously, this means that every time you come to an intersection you should be aware of all the different places from which cars and trucks (and motorcycles and bicycles) might emerge—and you should make sure the coast is truly clear before entering the intersection. It's also critically important to teach your child from a young age to think this way while riding.

Some of the vehicles that are about to occupy the same space that you and your child are rolling into could be invisible to you. They may be obscured by parked cars; they might be behind you, coming up swiftly to make a right turn. They may be hundreds of feet away, but moving fast and about to crank a left turn right across your line. Before entering the motorized realm, verify that the space will remain clear. It requires some mental work as well as looking around, more work than many riders would like to do while engaged in an activity that they consider carefree.

Often when riding on a sidewalk you are faced with the prospect of crossing in front of a car that is pulling out of a driveway or alley. Depending on which way you are rolling with respect to car traffic on the street, this can be a major hazard. If you are riding down the sidewalk in the same direction as traffic on your side of the road, then the driver pulling out will be looking toward you as you approach. However, if you're riding the opposite direction, against traffic, the driver will be looking the other way. It's pretty unrealistic to think that such a driver is going to swing her head around and check for bike or pedestrian traffic coming down the sidewalk, although she should.

Most often the driver sees a gap in the line of approaching vehicles and hustles the car into the street without a thought about people on the sidewalk. When bicyclists attempt to cross in front of cars driven by such drivers, they often get hit. This is easily preventable. Simply stop and wait for these drivers to complete their pull-out, or cross behind their vehicles. Just like that, you eliminate a lot of the danger of sidewalk riding.

Bike Paths

Family bikers would just as soon do all their riding on off-street bike paths, if that were somehow possible. It's undeniably comforting to ride where motor vehicles aren't. But the need for defensive riding doesn't vanish just because you're on a path. You might even find yourself putting your defensive skills to use quite often. The fact of the matter is that a jogger or another bicyclist can wreck you and your child just as easily as a car can.

Impatience is a dangerous disease on bike paths, or, more accurately, multi-use paths (MUPs). It's a factor in many of the crack-ups that occur there. With many different riders of varying abilities, all riding different speeds on a 10- to 15-foot-wide surface, along with joggers and dog-walkers, conflicts arise frequently. When a fast rider comes upon a slower rider, the fast rider can usually pass without much difficulty or fanfare. (When passing, announce yourself with a friendly "on your left" as you approach.) However, when riders are coming from the opposite direction and are on pace to pass the slow rider at the same time, the faster rider is faced with a choice: Slow and wait until the oncoming lane is clear to pass or speed like a maniac by the slower rider. Guess which one the fast rider is going to choose. That's right.

If you're new to this, you won't believe how often super-impatient cyclists take liberties with your personal safety on a busy path—even when you're carrying a child. If you're a passer, maybe you won't believe how often you pass others inconsiderately and dangerously, just to keep your speed up. If that's you, just slow down. Be patient! Lack of patience, unrealistic expectations, and plain old rudeness are the culprits here. In other words, the culprits are very human.

We can't control the actions of others, but we can prepare ourselves better to handle them. Start with lower expectations. Don't expect smooth sailing on multi-use paths or assume others will act with patience and consideration. That puts you in the proper frame of mind to anticipate passing conflicts before they occur and, if you're one of those faster riders, makes it easier to accept slowing down for others. Watch for the other common problems too: oncoming riders not watching where they're going and drifting into your path, and walkers and joggers making sudden turns across your path. Both of these can be alleviated with a bell, or your voice. Just as on the street, situational awareness allows you to stay one step ahead of trouble.

Use Lights

It's preferable not to ride at night with your kid. But sometimes you don't have much choice. This is especially true in winter when parents are leaving work and picking up kids from daycare as darkness falls. Dark rush hour is the worst rush hour.

Get a headlight and a flashing red taillight for any low-light riding. This is important equipment from a legal/liability standpoint should something happen, but also helps keep you out of trouble in the first place. Almost everywhere, it is illegal to ride a bike at night without lights. And it can't hurt to use lights in daylight too. If you're pulling a trailer, get an extra flashing taillight or two for the trailer.

Expensive lights do a good job of lighting up the road ahead and make you more visible to others. Low-cost lights, generally speaking, work fine to enhance visibility but don't do very well at enhancing vision. Frankly, though, you will probably be able to see where you're going just fine without an expensive headlight. Even if you're not on the street, a light is important equipment, alerting oncoming cyclists to your presence.

Things like reflective vests and lighting are icing on the cake for a defensive-minded bicyclist (see "Reflective Materials" on page 184). Defensive bikers use them. At the same time, they don't rely on them. They understand that some drivers aren't even watching the road. When a driver's eyes aren't pointed in the right direction, lighting is a non-issue. Defensive riders understand and ride accordingly.

Part Two:
EQUIPMENT

CHAPTER 5

Kids' Helmets

Catching Bea

Robert here. One of my top concerns as a stay-at-home dad to our new daughter Beatrice has been her propensity to topple over, suddenly and awkwardly, and whack her head on the floor, sidewalk, or table edge, whatever's closest and hardest. She seems to have a real talent for it. I'm told this is a thing with toddlers.

Those months when she was pulling herself up to her feet and trying to walk were particularly terrifying. Babies at this stage aren't very good at getting their hands out to break falls, and their heads are still massive relative to their bodies. I spent all my time shuffling along behind her, ready to catch. If I happened to turn away for a second, of course that was when she fell. Boom!

When we talked to our pediatrician about it, she tried to allay our fears. Toddlers are so tough, she said. She also mentioned that when her kid was that age, she broke down and *strapped a bike helmet on her while she was toddling around the house!* We all shared a hearty laugh. We had the same

Most parents would be surprised to learn that the liners of toddler bike helmets are made of the same materials, with the same density, as the liners of adult bike helmets. The Consumer Product Safety Commission, the agency that sets the standards, was not persuaded by arguments that kids' helmets should be softer than adult helmets. *Robert Hurst* thought many times. We should put a helmet on this kid! Of course we never followed through on it. Should we have? In the future will toddlers wear helmets around the house?

Even after Bea graduated from that wobbly stage, the cranial excitement continued. Once Christie was carrying her and stepped in an "inspection hole" that was left in the street by the gas company; she and Bea went slamming to the pavement, and Bea hit her head so hard that she lost consciousness. Fire trucks, ambulances. We spent the day at the ER where the doctors and nurses simply monitored Bea's outward signs to make sure she wasn't about to die. There was no follow-up or concern about long-term effects, but a lot of reassurance that everything was going to be a-okay.

I couldn't help noticing that our society, including the medical community, holds a rather blasé attitude toward these typical toddler head smacks, even though they can be deadly dangerous. They see them all the time. "That's toddlers for ya!" Meanwhile, the prospect of a bicycle-related knock on the head is among the ultimate bugaboos, right up there with abduction by candy-slinging strangers in white vans.

Weirdly, the societal pressure to outfit one's little bike passenger in a miniature helmet comes from all angles—news media, government agencies, doctors, bike people, random passersby—and never lets up. Meanwhile, pressure to protect your child's head in almost any of those other head-smacking situations is nonexistent, and would be laughed away if it did exist.

Americans have gone so far as to mandate, in many places around the country, that kids under a certain age wear helmets when riding or carried on bicycles. Imagine what people would say if a law were proposed mandating toddlers wear helmets around the house when learning to walk. And where are all the nonprofits and safety councils, the PSAs and pamphlets with their pleading to parents about household head injuries?

What's going on here? Why the double standard? If you're a conspiracy-minded dolt like me, you won't have to look too hard to find fuel for a theory or two.

Maybe the incredible amount of energy directed at parents about kids' bike helmets is appropriate. If that's true, however, then the failure to helmet our toddlers when not biking is a massive tragedy. Most likely, the truth is found somewhere in the middle—we could be more careful with our kids' heads in everyday situations, and we could think more critically about bike helmets at the same time.

In my opinion you could make a strong argument that mandatory helmet laws for adults are misguided and that much of the reverence for helmets these days is delusional, even dangerous in a way, for bicyclists' safety and overall community health. However, I have always felt differently about helmets for kids. It seemed to me that helmets are more appropriate for kids for several reasons. Kids are more likely to topple over and are more likely to hit their heads when they do. Furthermore, helmet testing parameters seem to indicate that the typical bike helmet—kids' or adults'—is designed to protect the head in the type of low-speed crash that is so disproportionately dangerous to little kids. Lately the Consumer Product Safety Commission, the agency responsible for regulating bike helmets, is telling us that assumption is false (see "Youth Helmet Standards: Scandalous?" below), that helmets are in fact designed for high-energy crashes and don't protect kids from concussions when they fall off their bikes.

For most people, there is no question or controversy about putting kids in bike helmets. But those of us who have really studied the issue and thought hard about it see a lot of unsolved mysteries and vexing dilemmas. It's not clear-cut at all.

I still think every kid who rides a bike or is carried on one, with the exception of infants in car seats, should wear a helmet. I'm not as convinced as the rest of America is with the typical helmet's protective properties—I won't shame parents who let their kid ride without—but I think the kid is

WHY NOT PLAYGROUND HELMETS?	
Estimated rate of all injury per 100,000 children ages 0–4, associated with different types of household products:	
Chairs, sofas, sofa beds	813.6
Playground equipment	353.7
Non-glass doors, panels	297.3
Desks, cabinets, shelves, racks	283.8
Cans, other containers	153.5
Bicycles and accessories	140.5
Trampolines	80.9

("NEISS Data Highlights, 2012," US Consumer Product Safety Commission, www.cpsc.gov//Global/Neiss_prod/2012NeissDataHighlights.pdf. The CPSC calculates injury rates per population using the US Census Bureau's July 1, 2012, US resident population estimates.)

probably better off with the helmet. You do what you can do with the tools at hand. Hopefully we can help make those tools more effective by calling more attention to the issue.

I make sure Bea is wearing her helmet whenever she's a passenger or riding her balance bike, which is often. Then, I don't rush to take the thing off when she gets in the house. It's dangerous in here.

Youth Helmet Laws

Twenty-one states and the District of Columbia have passed laws requiring kids, usually those under age 16 or 18, to wear helmets while riding bikes. Additionally, numerous towns, cities, and counties have mandated helmet use for kids.

This gets confusing for parents of small children. If a state or city has a law requiring helmets for all kids under, say, 16, does that law also cover toddler passengers riding on bikes ridden by their parents? Well, if you're in Connecticut, the answer is no. It is not required for passengers to wear helmets in Connecticut.[1] Whether this was on purpose, or the result of simple oversight, is unknown. Probably the latter. And we wouldn't be surprised if that soon changed in Connecticut too, because in every other helmet law state, passengers are explicitly required to wear helmets.

The Delaware Code is representative of the typical language found in these mid-1990s statutes: "A person under sixteen years of age shall not operate, ride upon, or ride as a passenger any [sic] bicycle, unless that person is wearing a properly fitted and fastened bicycle helmet which meets or exceeds the [outdated standards listed here]."

Delaware, like California, Florida, New Jersey, and Pennsylvania, goes so far as to specify that kids in trailers, and not just kids in seats, are included in the helmet law. The child helmet laws of Maine, Louisiana, Massachusetts, New Hampshire, New York, North Carolina, Oregon, Rhode Island, and Tennessee also include passengers on bicycles, but don't mention trailers, leaving ambiguity there. If you want to go helmetless in a trailer, you might get off on a technicality in these states.

Some of the states that don't mention trailers, like Tennessee and North Carolina, explicitly require that any child passenger under 40 pounds be strapped into a seat. Does that mean moving a small kid by trailer is illegal in Tennessee and North Carolina, helmet or not? We highly doubt that was the intent of lawmakers; we also doubt it has become the practical effect of the law. Most likely, the legislators hadn't contemplated the possibility of trailers at the time they wrote the laws, or had seen too few kids in trailers for it to make an impression. More recent online statements from the North Carolina Department of Transportation, for instance, mention trailers as if they were part of the law all along.

Georgia has an interesting law. They also include passengers in their under-16 helmet requirement but then depart from the typical line. The state explicitly allows children under 1 year to be carried in a sling or in a trailer—no mention of cargo bikes here—"so long as such child is seated in the bicycle trailer or carried in an infant sling according to the bicycle trailer's or infant sling's manufacturer's instructions," and as long as the baby is wearing a helmet! But remember, it is not a good idea for an infant to wear a helmet while strapped into a car seat or infant carrier of any kind, which is generally how parents move their small infants via bike trailer. The carrier *is* the helmet. This has been and will probably continue to be a difficult point to get across.

Child helmet laws are directed at you, not your toddler. Oregon has created a new crime for scofflaw parents who bike with unhelmeted children: The offense is endangering a bicycle passenger and is punishable by a fine of $25.

These state and local helmet statutes tend not to be hard-edged, draconian requirements. Fines and penalties are minimal. Often it is stated that a violation should result in no penalty whatsoever other than more persuasion to buy and use a helmet. More importantly, many of these statutes are accompanied by a statement that failure to wear a helmet cannot be used as evidence of negligence in case of a crash.

We recommend putting a certified helmet on your kid, and if you strap it on correctly, you're satisfying whatever sort of helmet law applies. But life isn't always that simple. Some parents want to bike with babies in secure infant carriers that don't work with helmets, for instance. Other folks—the entirety of Europe, for example—may not feel that a ride on quiet roads or paths really demands a crash helmet. There are little differences in the child helmet laws from state to state and town to town. If you feel the need, check your local laws by doing an Internet search for [state name] Revised Statutes, and [city] Traffic Code. You can find the bicycle-specific laws buried in the vehicle or traffic sections.

HOW TO GET YOUR TODDLER
TO WEAR A HELMET

You know how it goes. Everyone is ready for the family bike ride, or the commute to preschool, or the ramble to the park. Everyone is happy! Until one tiny person ruins it by having one of those inexplicable meltdowns where he does his stiff as a board/heavy as an anvil bit while shrieking like a fishwife, just because you told him to put a piece of styrofoam on his head. How do you convince your toddler to wear his helmet?

Like anything with toddlers, it's not an exact science. But there are a few things you can do to maybe make helmet wearing more consistently appealing. A two-pronged approach might work best. The first part is about buy-in—making your toddler invested in the helmet. The second is based on consequences and rewards.

1. Buy-In

When it comes time to purchase a helmet, bring your child with you and let her choose between a few different models that you have preapproved. If she wants the pink one with the unicorns, fine! If she wants the Minecraft creeper helmet, excellent. The important thing here is that she feels some ownership.

Parents are cautioned not to allow kids to put stickers on the shells of their helmets, for fear that the stickers might somehow mess up the protective qualities of the helmet. But as long as the stickers are paper-thin and don't have any extra texture, they won't cause any problems. If you think it will help, let your toddler decorate her helmet using stickers with characters from favorite shows or books. The stickers might make the helmet just appealing enough for your toddler to wear it, tantrum-free.

Let your kid see you wearing a helmet. Kids do pick up on what adults are doing. For instance, your child might notice how you always stop at the "wine store" on the way home on Friday evenings, and she even might start suggesting that you stop there on Thursday nights too. Likewise, she will probably make a mental note of your helmet wearing, which might make her want to wear one. The AAP makes it part of their official helmet recommendation: "Pediatricians should encourage parents to wear a helmet when bicycling to model safe behavior for their children."

(American Academy of Pediatrics, Committee on Injury and Poison Prevention, "Bicycle Helmets," *Pediatrics,* Vol. 108 No. 4, October 1, 2001, pp. 1030–32.)

Don't get overzealous about this, however. Adults can do what they choose within the law. That's the beauty of being an adult. Don't we tell kids to do all kinds of things that we don't do ourselves? Take naps, sit in car seats. Mommy drinks wine, baby doesn't. It would be a pretty nutty world if parents had to do everything that they're trying to get their kids to do.

Some kids who don't like to wear helmets may be pushed even further away from the idea if their parents don't wear them. But many kids like wearing helmets and don't seem to notice or care if their pedaling parent isn't wearing one. Remember: There are many ways to set an example for kids while riding a bicycle— wearing a helmet is only one.

2. Consequences and Rewards

If your toddler refuses to wear a helmet, the natural consequence could be that she can't go for a bike ride. Sorry kid: no helmet, no ride. This could be particularly effective if you are going somewhere optional yet fun. Like to the park. Or to get ice cream. This might not work if you are headed to the doctor to get your toddler a legful of shots.

You could mix in a reward with the purpose of your ride. Maybe you are headed out the door to go to the grocery store, but your toddler falls to the floor in helmet-related hysterics. Try suggesting to her that you combine the grocery store trip with something fun, like 10 minutes at the park. It might be enough to convince her to strap the helmet on.

When all else fails, there is always bribery. "I'll give you an M&M if you put your helmet on," can sometimes work. Or, if you want it to feel less like bribery and more like a finely crafted, B. F. Skinner–approved behavior plan, you can make a sticker chart. Every time your child dons his helmet without an argument, he gets a sticker on the chart. When he accumulates five (or ten, or whatever) stickers, he gets a prize. Bonus points if the prize is a bike ride!

Remember—satisfying a helmet law is just the tip-top of the safety iceberg. As we'll see below, putting a helmet on your kid could mean even less than cynics like us ever thought.

Youth Helmet Standards: Scandalous?

Since February 1999 all helmets sold in the United States have been subject to mandatory safety standards via the US Consumer Product Safety Commission (CPSC).[2]

The CPSC requires that any helmet sold in the United States must be able to pass a few tests. It must stay on the head ("positional stability"), it must not block the rider's peripheral vision within 105 degrees from the center of the helmet, and its retention system must be solid enough to stay intact under a modest amount of force; most importantly, it must be able to lessen a blow to the head by a certain amount. Any helmet must be able to pass specific impact tests in which it is strapped onto a "headform" and dropped in free fall onto a flat surface at about 14 miles per hour and a curb-like surface at 11 miles per hour. As measured by an accelerometer buried inside the headform, the helmet must be able to reduce the force of these blows from around 350g–400g to under 300g ("g" referring to gravity)— a modest reduction but a critical one according to some. Helmets in any given production lot must be able to achieve this under four very different conditions: at regular ambient conditions, at high temperatures, at low temperatures, and while soaked with water.

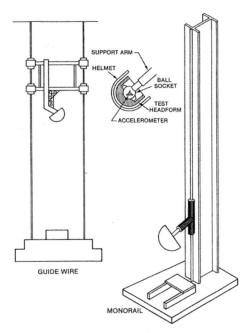

CPSC regulations require helmet manufacturers to test their products with a test apparatus that simulates modest falls onto various hard surfaces. Despite the obvious differences between kids' heads and adults' heads, the testing parameters and standards are the same for kids' helmets and adults' helmets. *Consumer Product Safety Commission*

Interestingly (or perhaps infuriatingly is a better word) the CPSC's impact standards are exactly the same for kids' helmets and adults' helmets, and they are tested using headforms of the same weight, despite the huge differences between kids' heads and adults' heads. Aside from a rule requiring more coverage on the sides and back, the CPSC allows manufacturers to produce helmets for toddlers that are just miniature versions of adult helmets, using the very same materials, which happen to be optimized for adult heads. Given the huge weight differences between a toddler's head and an adult's, and huge differences in their ability to withstand blows, this was a distressing decision when it was made back in the 1990s. Many who were party to the discussion felt strongly that kids' helmets should be tested with an appropriately weighted headform and should be able to reduce blows to under 250g.

Proponents of special provisions for young children's helmets believe that these helmets should be tested under different parameters than helmets intended for older persons. The current test parameters are based primarily on adult head injury tolerance and on a headform mass that is approximately that of an adult head. Supporters of special provisions contend that these adult test parameters result in a helmet with a liner that is too stiff to optimally protect a young child's head. By using a headform weight that better represents a young child's head (e.g., 8.6 lbs/3.9 kg), and reducing the allowable peak-g, helmets would need to be designed with a lower density (less stiff) liner to further lessen the impact transmitted to the head.[3]

From a mathematical standpoint, it was shown that reducing the stiffness of a helmet liner to account for the lighter head of the child could reduce injury in children, but it might also increase the severity of injury from really hard impacts that cause the liner to bottom out. To know for sure whether the proposed rules would benefit kids, or harm them, the CPSC studied how many kids had their injuries exacerbated by too-stiff helmets, and how many had injuries associated with bottomed-out helmets. They found many examples of bicyclists suffering head injuries while wearing helmets that did not compress upon impact, a clear sign that their helmet liners weren't soft enough. However, since the ages of these bicyclists were not specified, the CPSC decided that the data was not useful.[4]

This looks like a major error in logic. After all, if adults are suffering head injuries because their helmets are too hard even for them, then kids with lighter heads, using helmets made of the same materials, will also suffer these injuries. The facts were there, but the CPSC looked right past them.

Citing the alleged lack of data and their lingering fear that making the helmet liners softer could cause more harm than good, the CPSC scrapped the proposal to create different standards for kids' helmets. This was a very convenient ruling for the helmet makers, as it allowed them to continue making kids' helmets the exact same way they were making adults' helmets, only smaller.

All that sound and fury promoting child helmet usage—and the helmet companies and regulators can't even be bothered to provide kids' helmets that are optimized for kids. The industry and CPSC insist that adult helmet standards are *good enough* for kids. They say, in fact, that the standards produce helmets that are equally effective for toddlers, older children, and adults, something that seems impossible on its face, given the obvious and massive physiological differences.

We hope the regulations change. Standards should ensure that the tiny helmets that kids are harangued and cajoled into wearing—and compelled by law into wearing in many cases—are actually designed in the best way possible to protect *kids*. After all, the CPSC's helmet standards were developed and enacted in response to the Children's Bicycle Helmet Safety Act of 1994. The whole idea behind the law was to develop helmet standards that specifically address the risk of injury to children. Somehow, that didn't really happen.

The argument in defense of the standard goes like this: Big studies show that bicycle helmets certified under the CPSC's standards are effective at protecting kids' heads. So, no need to fix what ain't broke.

The most famous (or infamous) and mega-cited of these big studies took place in the late 1980s. Researchers looked at bike crash victims showing up at Harborview Medical Center in Seattle and saw that those who wore helmets suffered fewer head injuries than those who did not. The researchers repeated their experiment with more careful controls in the 1990s and came up with less impressive numbers but still very positive results for helmets. The results of both studies have been trumpeted across the land ever since.[5]

Few realize that the famous 1996 Harborview helmet study told us virtually nothing about the effectiveness of helmets for kids under 5, with their much smaller and softer heads, because there was only one injured toddler included in the data. Yup, one. Still, to this day the Harborview study is the primary evidence cited by those who say helmet standards work fine for tiny kids.

It's not just random, rogue parents like us calling out the CPSC and helmet manufacturers for inappropriate standards and sketchy logic. As the standards were being finalized, the CPSC received a letter from Jim Sundahl, senior engineer at Bell Sports and head chair of the Bicycle Helmet Task Group at the American Society for Testing Materials (ASTM). Sundahl was deeply disturbed by the CPSC's impending decision on youth helmets. "We [Bell] pioneered infant/toddler helmets beginning in the early '80s," he wrote. "Since then we have sold hundreds of thousands of infant/toddler helmets . . . all this time, with all these models, we have never seen an infant/toddler helmet that was anywhere near bottoming out. Moreover, I collected damaged infant/toddler helmets for several months in 1995. Not only did I not see bottomed-out helmets, I didn't see any helmet showing signs of crushing on the inside." No crushing, no energy absorbed. May as well wrap a piece of concrete sidewalk around your head.

By using an adult-weighted (5 kg) headform in the tests, Sundahl argued, the CPSC was setting up kids for unnecessary brain injuries. "The 5 kg headform that produces say 250 g's in the laboratory test would produce nearly 400 g's in an identical impact in the real world given the weight of real babies' heads."[6]

The ASTM weighed in officially with their own study of the youth helmet standard in 2014. Ultimately, ASTM's study found kids' helmets and the CPSC's justification of the standard to be inadequate. The conclusion is simple: "Impact protection for children requires a combination of material thickness and density to produce helmet liners that are 'softer' than those often used in present-day helmets."[7]

There has been a tacit admission from the CPSC itself that the current standards, in fact, don't work. At some point fairly recently, the commission began to make a startling claim in their helmet-related communications. On a CPSC webpage titled "Which Helmet for Which Activity," there is an interesting proclamation the likes of which we old-timers had never heard before from a government agency: "No helmet design has been proven to prevent concussions. . . . *Beware of claims that a particular helmet can reduce or prevent concussions.*" (emphasis CPSC's.)[8] Say what? Not only that, as this

YOUTH HELMET RECALLS

- About 70,000 cheap helmets were recalled in July 2000, for failing CPSC impact tests and labeling rules. Prior to being recalled the helmets were sold at Kmart for about a year, from April 1999 through March 2000, with labels stating "Meets CPSC & ASTM Standards78." Customers were instructed to return their helmets to Rand International for a full refund on their eight bucks. ("CPSC, Rand International Announce Recall of Bicycle Helmets," CPSC, July 5, 2000, Release #00-139, www.cpsc.gov/en/Recalls/2000/CPSC-Rand-International-Announce-Recall-of-Bicycle-Helmets/.)

- About 9,000 cheap kids' helmets by Cycle Express were recalled in 2000 for failing CPSC standards. The helmets were sold at Toys R Us for about $13, but customers who bought them were only offered a $7 refund, "which is the assessed value of the helmet." The value of the helmet was diddly-squat, Toys R Us. That's the whole problem. ("CPSC, Cycle Express Inc. Announce Recall of Bicycle Helmets," CPSC, July 5, 2000, Release #00-140, www.cpsc.gov/en/Recalls/2000/CPSC-Cycle-Express-Inc-Announce-Recall-of-Bicycle-Helmets/.)

- Nine thousand Schwinn-brand helmets were recalled in 2004 due to failure to comply with impact testing requirements. They were sold in Wal-Marts and Targets and other stores nationwide from January 2004 through July of the same year. ("CPSC, PTI Sports Inc. Announce Recall of Schwinn Toddler Bicycle Helmets," CPSC, August 19, 2004, Release #04-199, www.cpsc.gov/

official story emerged that helmets don't prevent concussions, we started to hear that they aren't designed to prevent concussions.[9] Instead they are supposedly designed to keep skulls together in high-energy collisions. It's exactly the opposite of the story we used to hear! That's all very convenient, isn't it? And why would I want to put my toddler in a helmet designed for an adult's high-speed impact, when my primary concern is that she will tumble off her balance bike and smack her head on the sidewalk?

When they made the rules for kids' helmets, the CPSC mentioned that they would revisit the standards if new evidence came to light that the

en/Recalls/2004/CPSC-PTI-Sports-Inc-Announce-Recall-of
-Schwinn-Toddler-Bicycle-Helmets-/.)

- In 2005 about a half-million children's helmets for sale in Target stores were recalled because some of the helmets didn't meet CPSC standards. The helmets were sold under the brand name Back Trails Jr., with the CPSC certification label, for about 15 months in Target stores. Customers were given Target gift cards in lieu of a refund. ("CPSC, Target Announce Recall of Back Trails Jr. Bicycle Helmets," CPSC, August 31, 2005, Release #05-252, www.cpsc.gov/en/Recalls/2005/CPSC-Target-Announce-Recall-of-Back-Trails-Jr-Bicycle-Helmets/.)

- Another big pile of youth helmets—more than 30,000—failed to meet CPSC standards for impact resistance in 2012, according to the agency. The bad helmets were sold all over the place from August 2006 through November 2011, with the CPSC certification sticker and the words "Little Tricky" on the side. The importer, Triple Eight Distribution, offered a full refund.

  Did you catch that? These substandard helmets were sold for five years before the CPSC got around to recalling them.

  Officially, no injuries were pinned on these substandard lids. ("Bicycle Helmets Recalled by Triple Eight Distribution Due to Risk of Head Injury," CPSC, January 6, 2012, Revised April 17, 2013, Release #12-082, www.cpsc.gov/en/Recalls/2012/Bicycle-Helmets-Recalled-by-Triple-Eight-Distribution-Due-to-Risk-of-Head-Injury/.)

standards were unsuitable. This new consensus, that helmets don't prevent concussions even in adults, should be enough to spark a reexamination.

To do the right thing by American kids and their parents, the CPSC should strengthen youth helmet standards by softening youth helmets. And let's not forget that the helmet companies can go right ahead and create better helmets for kids without a government agency forcing them to do so. Parents should at least have the choice of buying softer helmets that really do provide protection against the type of head injuries that little kids are most likely to have.

Substandard Helmets on the Market

Those who just learned that their kid's helmet was designed to slow down an adult head will probably be further overjoyed to find out that some kids' helmets on the shelf at the local mega-store wouldn't be able to pass those CPSC impact tests—but sport CPSC certification stickers anyway.

When announcing the new mandatory standards in 1999, then chairman of the CPSC Ann Brown declared: "Because of this new standard, families will know that the bike helmets they buy meet stringent federal requirements aimed at preventing head injuries."[10] Well . . .

In the fifteen years following the advent of the CPSC's certification program, parents bought hundreds of thousands of certified helmets from American retailers that did not meet CPSC standards, according to the CPSC itself.[11] How did this happen? The answer lies in the fine print of the regulations, which allow the helmet companies to test and certify their own products. In fact the regulations allow helmet importers like Giro and Bell to rely on the good word of their manufacturers in China that such tests have been performed.

All this will probably come as a surprise to those who, like us, figured that the stickers were bestowed like combat medals by the agency whose name is emblazoned all over them, *after* tests performed by the same agency. Nope. The manufacturers print up the stickers themselves, no testing by the CPSC required. The CPSC barely exists in material form at this point in the helmet-selling process; it is little more than an abstract set of arcane rules, floating in the ether. Even if the agency gets around to performing its own tests, the helmets are already in the stores.

The history of CPSC helmet recalls since the standards were implemented is not exactly encouraging. It shows that the agency is working to get noncompliant helmets off the market, but it also proves that the rules don't prevent noncompliant helmets from entering the market in the first place. In some cases they not only enter the market but stay there a long time.

The Big Mystery

Let's think about this for a second or two. Hundreds of thousands of bike helmets were purchased that didn't meet CPSC standards for one reason or another. Kids wore them, and despite the recalls they're still wearing them. The chance that a parent will hear about one of these recalls is pretty small.

Nobody from the government is going to come over to the house and tell them about it.

With all those bad helmets floating around, there must be a lot of suffering as a result. Many unnecessary and tragic head injuries. Right? That's a lot of bad helmets. But apparently not. In fact, according to the CPSC's own recall notices, not one single injury has ever been pinned on any of these recalled helmets. "No injuries reported."

Something is not right here. If there are real injuries being caused by these substandard helmets, they're being kept quiet. If there are no bad outcomes associated with hundreds of thousands of substandard helmets, then helmet certification and testing can't possibly matter that much. Why do we even bother?

It's an interesting thing. We're not supposed to think too hard about it.

Buyers' Guide

So what can parents do to avoid picking up a substandard helmet, given the massive loopholes in the regulations and the CPSC's seemingly tardy enforcement?

First, we recommend buying a helmet "made by" a reputable helmet company. We put "made by" in quotes because as far as we can tell, none of these companies actually make their own helmets. It would be more accurate to call them distributors or importers, rather than makers. The helmets are all made in Chinese factories.

When you buy a helmet from one of the big name companies, like Bell, Giro, or Razer, at least then you know you're dealing with a brand that has a lot to lose, should some horrible scandal arise. We think these are the companies that are most likely to actually test the helmets they sell and to exercise careful quality control. For such a helmet, you're going to pay a little more ($30 to $60 as opposed to $20-ish), and you might have to go to a bike shop to get it.

We would avoid picking up a cheap helmet at a "big box" store, as convenient as it might seem. Most of the recalls listed above involve discount helmets from no-name companies, sold at big box stores. In general it's a good idea to get bike-related stuff from bike shops, or at least from sporting goods stores that have strong bike departments. If the same dude who put together your kid's bike is also in charge of lawn chairs and gas grills, that's a bad sign.

Before you buy, measure your child's head with a cloth tape measure, just above the ears. If the circumference isn't yet 17 inches or so, you won't find a helmet small enough to fit. In that case you might choose to transport the kid in a child seat strapped into a *bakfiets* or trailer.

Fit is arguably the most important aspect of a bike helmet. When it's on your kid's head, the helmet should sit an inch or so above the eyebrows and should be close to level, not tipped back. Keep in mind that a slightly large helmet might fit just fine with thicker pads. We've listed sizes below, but take these numbers with a grain of salt. Frankly we've found some contradictory information from manufacturers and retailers about just how big these helmets really are, and we haven't measured them ourselves.

Different brands have different retention systems and fit characteristics—meaning helmets of the same alleged size could fit quite differently. The best thing to do is take your kid to a shop with several different types and try them on, see which fits best. This will also give your kid a chance to choose a style she likes. The whole helmet thing can be pretty fun for kids.

Helmets are made a few different ways. Your typical cycling-style helmet will either have a plastic shell glued onto the expanded polystyrene (EPS) that forms the meat of the helmet, or will be "in-molded," a more advanced process taking over in the industry in which the shell and EPS are fused together in the mold. Both types are said to be built to the same standards. The old-school helmet with the stuck-on shell may start to come apart a little earlier.

You could also get a helmet with a skate-inspired look provided it's also (cough) certifiably crash-tested for bike riding. (Helmet companies aren't supposed to market a helmet for use while bicycling unless it can pass the CPSC's tests for bicycle helmets.) With hard shells and padding inside, these skate/BMX-style helmets have a completely different design, but are said to protect the head just the same. Go with your kid's style preference, as it will make it much easier to get him to wear the thing.

Think about the weight of the helmet—the lighter the better for young kids. Also consider the potential for overheating when choosing your kid's helmet, though venting should be more subdued on a child's model. Vents probably make it more likely that the wearer's neck will get twisted upon impact. Also, any kids' helmet should have some sort of reflective properties.

Note that some youth helmets are available with MIPS (Multi-directional Impact Protection System) technology. MIPS helmets are designed to reduce rotational forces from off-center impacts. This is an important advance in helmet technology, but it's geared more toward high-speed riders and high-energy crashes. A MIPS helmet would make more sense for an older kid or a toddler transported on the back of an adult's bike than it would for a toddler cruising on a balance bike at low speeds.

Product List

Bell Octane. $40. 50–57 centimeters (19.75–22.5 inches). (1 size). 310 grams (11.2 ounces). Cycling style.

Bell Trigger. $35. 50–57 centimeters (19.75–22.5 inches). (1 size). 271 grams (9.5 ounces). Cycling style. 23 vents.

Bell Zipper. $35. 47–54 centimeters (18.5–21.25 inches). (1 size) 271 grams (9.5 ounces). Cycling style.

Giro Dime. $40. 18.5–21.75 inches (47–55 centimeters). (2 sizes). 410 grams (14.3 ounces). Skate/BMX style. MIPS model available.

Giro Me2. $30. 18.75–20.5 inches (48–52 centimeters). (1 size). 240 grams (8.5 ounces). Cycling style.

Giro Rascal. $40. 18–21.5 inches (46–54 centimeters). (2 sizes). 288 grams (10.1 ounces). Cycling style. Flashing lights on the back.

Giro Raze. $45. 19.75–22.5 inches (50–57 centimeters). (1 size). Cycling style. With 22 vents.

Giro Rodeo. $30. 19.75–21.75 inches (50–55 centimeters). (1 size). Cycling style.

Lazer BOB. $26. 46–52 centimeters (18–20.5 inches). 275 grams (9.5 ounces). Cycling style. Flat back works well in some trailers and seats.

Lazer Nut'z. $49. 50–56 centimeters (20–22 inches). 300 grams (10.5 ounces). Cycling style. MIPS model available.

Lazer P'Nut. $49. 46–50 centimeters (18–20 inches). 270 grams (9.5 ounces). Cycling style. MIPS model available.

Nutcase Baby Nutty. $45. 47–50 centimeters (18.5–19.6 inches). (1 size). 280 grams (9.8 ounces). Skate/BMX style.

Nutcase Little Nutty. $60. 48–52 centimeters (19–20.5 inches). (1 size). 400 grams (14 ounces). Skate/BMX style.

Specialized Small Fry. $40. 47–55 centimeters (18.5–21.75 inches). Cycling style. Flat back works well in some trailers and seats.

Specialized Small Fry Toddler. $40. 44–52 centimeters (17.5–20.5 inches). Cycling style. Flat back works well in some trailers and seats.

Uvex Hero. $50. 49–55 centimeters (19.2–21.6 inches). 205 grams (7 ounces). Cycling style. Unique pinch-free buckle. Uvex helmets are certified under European regs instead of CPSC and may be difficult to obtain in the United States.

CHAPTER 6

Front Seats

See the World

Who doesn't like sitting in the front row?

Front-mounted seats have become vastly more popular as active parents discover how easy they are to use and how much their kids love to ride in these things. The front position gives the child a better view, more excitement, and better communication with the parent than any other family biking method.

Jonathan Maus tried several different methods of family biking and liked the Bobike front seat best of all. "It's really great to have the kids up front and so close to the embrace of my arms. We can talk and share the sights and sounds of the road, unlike having them stuffed back in a trailer or typical child seat over the rear rack."

Another biking mother agreed with that sentiment. "There's nothing quite like the front seat for carrying a kid. It's a special way to travel for both child and parent."

As with the rear seat, a child in the front seat needs to be able to hold herself up reasonably well. No hopeless slumpers. We recommend waiting until the child can hold her head up well with a helmet on. That puts the minimum age for a front seat at about 9 months. The lawyers for European child seat manufacturers are comfortable with stating a minimum age of 9 months for using their products. Deciding they needed more CYA, the

Americans went along with CPSC and AAP recommendations, setting their magic number at 1 year.

Many parents have safely and successfully carried younger babies, unhelmeted, in front child seats. But we strongly recommend carrying younger babies in car seats that are strapped into trailers or cargo bike boxes (see "Riding with Infants" on page 18).

Don't worry too much about the manufacturers' age guidelines, but pay careful attention to the weight limits. When your little bundle of joy breaks 35 pounds or so, they've outgrown the front seat. That limit gives you around a two-year window to use the front seat, maybe. You can move them to a rear seat for a while longer, but soon you'll have to find another method.

Riding with a child mounted essentially on your handlebars may seem like a nutty idea, but it's surprisingly easy. Since the invention of the "safety bicycle," cyclists have understood that carrying a load over the front of the bike preserves the machine's maneuverability in a nice way. It feels good, strangely. In the history of cycling, pro delivery people have consistently chosen to place loads over the front wheel rather than the rear. But it still makes a comfortable old bike feel very different, which can be disconcerting.

The most commonly mentioned negative of the front-mounted seat is interference with pedaling. The front seat likes to make contact with legs and various other body parts during tight turns, thus hindering the rider's ability to make these turns. A pedaling parent might even have to stick the knees out pretty far just to ride straight. The severity of this problem will depend on the bike, the rider, and the seat in question, some of which are worse than others in this regard. This interference can be disconcerting and, during those first few rides when you're getting used to the equipment, potentially dangerous. After you figure it out, it's a simple annoyance at worst.

Are Front Seats Dangerous?

Consumer Reports delivered an a priori verdict against all bike-mounted child seats: "A child would have a fall of about 3 feet from a mounted bike seat, which increases the possibility and potential severity of an injury."[1] So along with a lot of the High Priests of Safety, *Consumer Reports* recommends parents use trailers instead of child seats, front or back.

Front seats provide pleasant and casual biking for parent and child.
Pixfly/iStock/Thinkstock

MAMA-CHARI

In the cities of Japan, space is at a premium. Ownership of private vehicles is impractical and curtailed. People in Japan utilize transit or go about their daily travels on foot or on bicycles, at a far greater rate than typical Americans. They leave their cars at home or decline to own cars at all. Families are used to getting around on bicycles.

For practical and geographical reasons, and probably some cultural reasons we don't understand, Japanese family bikers, almost exclusively, carry their children in seats mounted on their bicycles. They have even developed a special sort of bicycle that is designed especially for transporting shopping bags and multiple kids in child seats: the *mama-chari*. Roughly translated, the "mama chariot."

Japanese mama chariots are equipped with several features that make them incredibly practical tools for family biking. Typically these family bikes are equipped with slightly smaller front wheels to facilitate cargo and kid carrying up front. A step-through frame makes the rider's life easier and adds safety for passengers too. Mama-chari come equipped with generator lights, fenders, racks, and chain cases. Crucially, they have sturdy *bakfiets*-style double kickstands attached to the rear wheel. Also, according to one observer, "brakes that go 'SCREEEEEEEEEEEECH!' when even slightly feathered, startling everyone within earshot." (Byron Kidd, "Introducing the Mamachari," Tokyo By Bike [website], June 23, 2009, www.tokyobybike.com/2009/06/introducing -mamachari.html.)

Part of the practical genius of the mama-chari lies in the riding habits of Japanese cyclists and the cultural expectations assigned to different road users in Japan. In Japanese towns, bicyclists commonly use the sidewalks, despite the lack of space to be found there. It would be extremely difficult or impossible to pull a child in a trailer through the pedestrians on Japan's city sidewalks. The Northern European options like the bakfiets and cargo trike didn't catch on in Japan either, being just too unwieldy. Even the long-tail cargo bikes so popular in the United States are probably too large to fit nicely into Japan's traffic mix. But the mama-chari are relatively maneuverable—essentially regular bikes optimized to carry seats and baskets, rather than behemoth rigs built to carry a few hundred extra pounds.

Mama-chari are also amazingly cheap, costing maybe 20,000 yen for a higher-end model (about $200). A typical Japanese family doesn't want to spend thousands of dollars on a big cargo bike and treat it like another member of the family, the way Portlanders do. They don't romanticize their mama-chari too much. They simply use them, and use them hard. They don't bother bringing them inside or protecting them from the elements. When the bike falls into disrepair, they're about as likely to buy a new one as they are to fix the old one. When their bikes are stolen, they don't lose any sleep over it.

It ain't sexy. Or is it? Well, the Japanese don't think so. They're just trying to get from here to there and back. The rest of us, however, might be eyeballing these mama-chari with lust in our hearts.

In recent years bike sellers outside Japan have connected the dots between the low, low price of mama-chari bicycles and the rapidly rising demand for kid-carrying cargo bikes in England and the United States. One entrepreneur in London imported hundreds of used mama-chari bikes in 2013, reconditioned them, and sold them for about twice what they cost new in Japan. The guys on the Japan side of these deals watched in amazement. "They couldn't quite understand why someone in Britain, which pioneered bicycles, would be interested in buying such low-grade utility machines." (William Hollingworth, "Used 'mamachari' popular in London," *Japan Times*, November 11, 2013, www.japantimes.co.jp/news/2013/11/15/national/used-mamachari-popular-in-london-2/#.VDB06IxOTwI.)

In the United States the potential for a hipster feeding frenzy on genuine mama-chari bikes remains unexploited at the time of this writing.

Possibility and potential. Looks potentially, possibly bad to all reasonable parties. Who hasn't fallen off a bicycle at some point in their lives? We can easily imagine how a simple wipeout could be disastrous for a young passenger in a seat.

Front child seats were completely invisible in the United States until recent years. Any sort of decent research on the danger of child seats is old research, generally, produced when nobody in the United States used front-mounted seats. Since front and rear seats are substantially different, and likely have different danger profiles (to completely make up an official-sounding term), the old research is not completely useful when applied to front seats. We'll look more closely at that research in our discussion of rear seats in the next chapter.

When you're riding with your child in a seat in front of you, it doesn't feel all that dangerous. You're probably going to be riding pretty slowly. You're going to be extra averse to risks. And if you do fall, the kid is between your arms.

As with the rear seat, much of the danger involves those moments when the kid is in the seat, but you're not on the bike. In these moments the bike could topple over with the kid in the seat, a very dangerous thing. If there's one thing we'd like people to take away from this book, it's an understanding of this possibility. The old research shows that this is a major problem, accounting for a high percentage of seat-related injuries (and making the danger of actually riding in a child seat seem worse than it really is). See the next chapter for more on that.

Don't trust a single-leg kickstand. Don't rely on one when your child is up there. If you really want to do the child seat thing right, use a double-leg cargo bike kickstand, like the Japanese mothers on their *mama-chari* bikes.

Buyer's Guide

Front seats are smaller and cheaper than rear seats, but at $100-plus still cost more than we'd like. There aren't many models available in the United States right now, but those that are should be easy to find. You won't have to summon distributors with a Ouija board. The manufacturers of front-mounted child seats must be doing pretty well.

Stop! Before you buy, make sure the seat will work with the bike you plan to use. Front child seats can't be installed on all bikes. In general they are made with old-school Dutch-style city bikes in mind. The more sleek, modern, and American your bike is, the more trouble you will have attaching a front child seat to it. There usually needs to be some handlebar stem showing on which to attach the seat. So front seats are easier to install on old-school quill stems. If your bike has a threadless headset, you may need to get an adapter. Front seats may not work with drop bars.

Front seats can be accessorized with windscreens. Most models come with little "steering wheels," which give the child something to do with his hands.

Product List

Bobike Mini. $99. Weight capacity: 33 pounds. Windscreen available. Bobike is coming out with some new models with better straps and a slightly different seat design, but they're not yet available in the United States as the book goes to press.

Bobike Mini City. $128. Weight capacity: 33 pounds. Includes handlebar. Windscreen available.

iBert Safe-T-Seat. $110. Weight capacity: 38 pounds. Includes padded steering wheel.

Yepp Mini. $160. Weight capacity: 33 pounds. With built-in handlebar. Windscreen available.

The Yepp Mini front child seat *Courtesy Yepp*

Trade-Offs

Advantages: Easy to use; kids love it. Gives parents the ability to communicate and share experiences with their little passenger. Great for casual cruising.

Disadvantages: Can interfere with pedaling and steering; lack of support for child's head. Potentially more dangerous than trailers or box bikes.

CHAPTER 7

Rear Seats

Real and Imagined Dangers

The bicycle-mounted child seat comes with a lot of responsibility. If you mess up, it could cause serious injury to your kid. With the consequences of common and, to some extent, expected screw-ups amplified so much, users of child seats should ride more slowly and deliberately than they would otherwise. And, of course, the vast majority of family riders already understand that.

What's meant by "expected screw-ups?" For instance, running into a curb or pothole while turning your head to check for traffic. That's a classic, but there is much variety within this set of rider-induced mishaps. The slide-out on gravel, the flail and fall at low speed, the front wheel caught in a crack . . . These are the kinds of things that cause the vast majority of biking injuries. Which is also to say, the vast majority of biking injuries are pretty minor.

The occasional solo wipeout is a normal and expected part of bicycling, but when we're carrying kids we'd like to make such learning experiences as infrequent as humanly possible. It pays to have a good understanding of surfaces and how a bike works on them when you take your precious nugget out in a child seat.

"Riding in a bicycle-mounted child seat exposes the child to adult-level forces," researchers Robert Tanz and Katherine Christoffel reminded the

world in 1991.[1] Like the world needed any reminding. People were already forming very negative opinions about child seats by 1991. A cultural consensus was forming. It held that the child seat was an old-fashioned, leftover method of hauling children that was—obviously—too dangerous to be used by responsible parents. This consensus, bolstered by the usual voices of authority, lasted for a long twenty years or more before the latest batch of biking parents started to chip away at it.

People understand intrinsically that it could be dangerous to carry your child in a seat on the back of your bike. But, as always, it's best to keep things in perspective. Holding your child in your arms while standing also exposes her to the possibility of a bigger fall than her body can easily withstand. Putting your toddler in a car seat and getting on the highway exposes your child to forces that

The Bobike City rear child carrier *Courtesy Bobike*

are far beyond "adult-level forces." Doing so potentially exposes your child to forces that few adults could withstand. But, for some reason, nobody is going to tell you not to do that.

Looking for hard numbers on child seat–related crashes and injuries is almost a non-starter. There have been only a few big studies over the decades. The best known and probably the most useful was undertaken by Elizabeth Powell and Robert Tanz in 1999.[2] For this study the authors searched through data from the US Consumer Product Safety Commission's National Electronic Injury Surveillance System (NEISS) to find the relative risk of carrying a child in a trailer versus a rear seat. Their endeavor was fundamentally flawed, however, because of particular limitations in locating injuries involving trailers. As the authors note, "Some injuries related to bicycle-towed trailers may not be identified as there is no specific product code for them." That sure puts a damper on the comparing. So, while they found many times more seat-related injuries than injuries known to be related to trailers, this

Traditional rear-mounted child seats make family biking easy and fun and are a common sight in car-free areas of Barcelona. *Robert Hurst* discrepancy could have more to do with search limitations than anything else. It's impossible to say. Data about child seat injuries were clearer.

Powell and Tanz estimated that about 2,000 or so kids were taken to ERs with child seat–related injuries from 1990 through 1998. On the face of it, this looks pretty bad. But dig around a little bit. Turns out that more than half of those injuries occurred when the bike tipped over without the rider on it! More on that hugely important finding below. And 20 percent or so were spoke mishaps—a kid's hand or foot found its way into the spokes. Spoke injuries are more of an old-fashioned thing; modern seats effectively prevent it. These are very dangerous incidents and parents should work hard to avoid them, but they aren't examples of bike-seated kids being injured in crashes, which is what our fear is all about. Of those 2,000 or so injuries, about 500 were crash-related. That's about fifty crashes per year that were scary enough the parents took their kids at least to be checked out in the ER afterward.

Dig a little deeper. A relatively small percentage of those ER visits would have resulted in the child being admitted to the hospital with a serious injury. Not to belittle the kids who get hustled off to the ER or the parents who hustle them off, but that's how it works. The bulk of the injuries were likely minor at best. Or mostly imaginary. It's a proven pattern. It doesn't mean that all parties don't have PTSD after a very frightening crash, or that going to the ER wasn't a good idea.

We can only extrapolate from the available data, but the total number of serious, crash-related child seat injuries was something like ten or twenty per year nationwide in the 1990s. For the sake of simplification, we can assume that the numbers are similar a few decades later. Or we can admit that our almost complete lack of up-to-date information ultimately keeps us in the dark.

A dozen serious injuries per year. To put that in perspective, the number of serious injuries related to stairs is about 500 or 1,000 times larger.[3] The number of kids seriously injured while being transported in automobiles is astronomical in comparison. We understand that doesn't prove anything about the relative danger of these activities, but it does show that there is a wildly disproportionate focus on preventing a tiny number of injuries.

Compensating for the Risk

So the doctors' groups and various safety nanny organizations have a long-standing bad habit of playing up the danger of carrying kids in bike seats, ignoring actual evidence, and it's really short-sighted. Questions remain. One: Why are these groups exaggerating the danger of cycling with kids? This is a snarly question that we probably won't be able to answer in this book. But it's interesting to wonder about if you've got the time. Two: Why is the safety record of bike seats so surprisingly good? We have some thoughts on that one.

Risk compensation looms very large here. It could be precisely our overwrought fear of bike seats, a fear that permeates even the parents who use them, that puts riders in a state of mind that keeps them out of trouble. With the kid on the back of the bike, parents become hypervigilant. And that's the best way to be if you want to avoid crashes and collisions. Not only vigilant—situationally aware and anticipating the mistakes of others—but riding slowly and deliberately as well. Riding as a conscious adult, not the daydreaming hellion that most of us have been on the bike at one time or another. Parents won't dart into gaps in traffic, jump curbs, corner at the edge of traction, or charge down rough dirt trails with their kids riding along.

So riders tend to act in a much safer manner with a kid on the bike. That's pretty obvious stuff. Less obviously, crashing with a child in a bike seat may simply be a lot less dangerous than people have always assumed, for various reasons.

Beyond modifying your own behavior, remember to use a seat with a high back and a good harness, and make sure the child is wearing a properly fitting helmet. (See the "Kids' Helmets" chapter.) There is some evidence that using a seat belt without a high-backed seat could actually increase the acceleration of the child's head in a crash. The high back is really important.[4]

Any time you're hauling a kid on the bike itself, it's absolutely critical that the child is situated so she can't get her feet caught in the spokes. Any good child seat will do this job for you with some kind of barrier between the kid's lower limbs and the wheel, as well as a system that keeps the feet strapped somewhat securely in place. If any of these elements is missing, don't use the seat. (Look for a seat that meets ASTM International safety standard F1625, which covers the spoke-shielding properties and materials of rear-mounted seats.)

The Hidden Danger of Child Seats

Even in limited studies we can find very interesting patterns, and the Powell-Tanz study is no exception. Particularly striking is their finding that *over half*

ANECDOTES: CHILD SEATS IN COURT

Anecdotal evidence is often compelling and adds to our information on a subject. The danger with anecdotal evidence, of course, is that it often gives a false impression of what is actually going on. If we're not careful, it could lead us to strategies that aren't helpful, or that are even harmful. Such misdirected activism is a real problem, seen disturbingly often in cycling advocacy. Read on with this in mind.

Court cases are an interesting place to look for anecdotal evidence about bike crashes. As you might expect, the number of bike-related cases that involve child passengers is small by any measure; relative to the total number of bicycle-related cases, it's minuscule. That's a good sign for us. When we dug up some cases that involved bike-mounted child seats, we noticed an encouraging pattern. Here are some examples:

On a typical morning in New York City, a woman is riding her bike on East Sixth Street, on her way to the daycare center. Her 3-year-old son is in a seat on the back of the bike. Suddenly a garbage truck swoops by and strikes the handlebar, throwing the bike, rider, and one small passenger roughly to the pavement. The mother sustains multiple injuries to her head, neck, face, and back, and is hospitalized. The child . . . not injured. (*Hall v. City of New York*, 2013 NY Slip Op 31870–NY: Supreme Court 2013, http://

of seat-related injuries occurred when the bike fell over while stationary. That's the blockbuster result of this research, in our opinion.

Those moments of putting your kid into the seat and taking him out could be among the most dangerous of the entire ride. These can be sketchy maneuvers. If the bike isn't securely held in the upright position, it could topple over with your kid in the seat. Avoiding this usually means relying on a kickstand of some kind. The traditional single-shaft kickstand that sits on one side of the bike and props it up at an angle might work, but it's a fundamentally precarious system, an off-kilter three-legged dance. Far better is the motorcycle-style kickstand with pegs on both sides, aka the double kickstand, like you'll find on cargo bikes or Japanese *mama-chari* bikes. It will hold the bike securely and straight up, making your life much easier and your child much safer.

scholar.google.com/scholar_case?case=2081107070088475846& q=bicycle+child+seat&hl=en&as_sdt=4006&as_ylo=2010.)

A man is cruising around his small town with his 3-year-old in a seat on the back of his bike, when he runs smack into a crossbeam—with his face. The collision destroys the man's face and bicycle. His child is completely uninjured. (*Poerio v. State of New York*, 144 AD 2d 129–NY: Appellate Division., 3rd Department, 1988, http://scholar.google.com/scholar_case?case=1388 4282071101954365&q=%22child+seat%22+AND+bicycle&hl=en &as_sdt=4006.)

Summer in Chicago. A man puts his 2-year-old kid in a bike seat and starts riding on sidewalks toward the Lincoln Park Bike Path. He wipes out hard on a raised lip in the concrete and breaks his hip in the crash. The child is unhurt. (*Lipper v. City of Chicago*, 600 NE 2d 18–III: Appellate Court, 1st District, 1st Division, 1992, http://scholar.google.com/scholar_case?case=418301361094753 9573&q=%22child+seat%22+AND+bicycle&hl=en&as_sdt=4006.)

These anecdotes line up with other child seat stories we have heard from parents. They are at once frightening and reassuring. We think one thing they might be telling us is that rear child seats, when used properly, aren't necessarily as dangerous as commonly believed. A good seat with a secure harness will offer some protection to the child in case of a crash.

Unfortunately the double kickstand tends not to be included among the standard components of bicycles sold in the United States. They are widely available, however, and easy to install.

The truth is you don't need a kickstand at all. If necessary you can hold the bike up with your legs as you put the child in the seat. This could actually be safer than using a single-leg kickstand, because there won't be any assumption on your part that the bike will stay upright on the kickstand, an assumption that is pretty dangerous. You prop the bike up, turn away for a second, casually satisfied that the kickstand will do its job, and the next thing you know the bike's crashing to the ground. At least this way you won't be letting go and turning away from the bike.

Whatever you do, don't lean the bike up against a wall or pole or anything else to get the child in and out of the seat. That's sort of the worst of both worlds, and the most likely method to end in disaster. In any case it's clear that the trailers own this one safety aspect of biking with babies and toddlers.

The kickstand issue should make it immediately apparent that some bikes are better suited than others for hauling a kid in an attached child seat. Beyond the double kickstand, the ultimate child seat bike would certainly have a step-through frame. That is, it would be a "girl's bike." In the 1890s women's frames were made to accommodate long skirts. Now we understand that not having a top tube to mess around with is good for safety and makes a bike easier to use. This is especially true when carrying a kid in a child seat.

Handling the Bike

From a handling standpoint the rear-mounted seat shines in tight urban settings, in our opinion. Not everybody shares that opinion, mind you. But we like the way a solid bike feels with a kid on the back, the prowess at low speeds and in sharp turns. It can feel very top-heavy at first, but once you get the hang of the thing—and it doesn't take long—you'll probably appreciate the handling characteristics of the bike with your kid on it. (As long as you don't have to go up any real hills.) Those who have added a child seat to a favorite bike that has snazzy handling may be uncomfortable for a while trying to get the feel of the new rig.

In our opinion it's difficult to pick a clear winner in the handling department between front and rear seats. Even though the load feels a little better over the front of the bike, the rear seat won't interfere with your ability to pedal or turn the handlebars sharply.

Negotiating tight spaces does require some extra care with a rear-mounted seat, however. Note that making a turn too close to a pole, pedestrian, or corner of a building could cause your seated child to collide with the object even if your body clears it. As with a semitruck, the track of the rear tire will always be inside the track of the front tire—closer to the apex of the turn.

Another issue becomes apparent when standing out of the saddle. If you're the type of rider who likes to stand on the pedals and whip the bike back and forth when climbing hills, you should know that doing so with your kid in the seat could give her a seriously unpleasant, whiplashy ride. Best to tone down the side-to-side thrashing; instead, stay seated or stand without rocking too much. The best way to affect this change is to use a smaller (easier) gear. Also, secure the seat at around the ergonomically correct height for pedaling. Putting the seat down low can feel casually nice and can give a feeling of security during low-speed maneuvering, but it also impedes your ability to get the most out of your pedal stroke, messes up your knees, and makes it more likely that you will want to stand up on the pedals.

Still considered by many in the United States to be an outmoded and unsafe method of transporting a child, the rear-mounted seat is making a comeback. It's no wonder, as it really does work well. Despite occasional issues with installation and compatibility with certain types of bikes, a good rear-mounted seat remains one of the best ways to bike with a toddler on board.

Buyer's Guide

Choosing a child seat that is compatible with your bicycle is a notoriously fiddly project, depending on the bicycle in question. In general the classic "Dutch bike" (the sort of old-school bike that Americans might call a "3-speed") will accept just about any seat. At the other end of the spectrum, mountain bikes with 29-inch wheels are incompatible with several models. In between, you'll find a variety of issues, most of which can be solved easily, some of which will be more frustrating.

Some of the cheaper seats are notorious for inadequate clearance and lack of adjustability, and have been left off the product list below, which is sad, because good seats are surprisingly expensive. It's impressive to see rear-mounted seats with $200-plus price tags—comparable to trailers that can carry two kids plus groceries and other cargo.

Most of the reputable child seats can be purchased with either of two main mounting systems: rack-mounted and frame-mounted. Both have their strong points. The common frame-mounted (generally seat tube–mounted) seats work very well. They're plenty secure, when attached properly, and provide more suspension than rack-mounted seats. It's okay for the seat to be a little bit bouncy, and it should be a little laid back too, not straight up and down.

If you fancy a rack-mounted seat, know that it will work best on a bike that has rack bosses (eyelets brazed onto the frame, to which the rack is bolted). Without the bosses, you'll get diminishing returns as you work on fitting the rack where it wasn't necessarily meant to fit. If you already have a rack and want to use a seat with it, make sure the seat you purchase is compatible with

CHILD SEAT RECALLS

- Schwinn Deluxe Bicycle Child Carriers, manufactured in China for PTI Sports, Inc., were recalled in 2006 after five reported incidents in which improperly installed seats broke and fell off, causing "bumps and scratches." The lack of serious injuries associated with this defect could be seen as more anecdotal evidence that bike seats offer surprisingly good protection to children in crashes. Customers were instructed to stop using the seats and to send away for a safety bracket. ("Bicycle Child Carriers Recalled Due to Fall Hazard," CPSC, May 9, 2006, Release #06-159, www.cpsc.gov/en/Recalls/2006/Bicycle-Child-Carriers-Recalled-Due-to-Fall-Hazard/.)

- About 40,000 Topeak Babyseat II bicycle carrier seats were recalled in 2012 for a different sort of hazard. The design of the seat's "grab bar" made it possible for a child's fingers to get caught in the hinge. Two incidents involving badly injured fingers were reported. Customers were instructed to stop using the seats and send away for a "free hinge cover retrofit kit." It's definitely something you'll want to think about if you're using one of these popular Topeak brand seats built before 2013. ("Todson Recalls Bicycle Child Carrier Seats Due to Laceration and Fingertip Amputation Hazards," USCPSC, April 5, 2012, Release #12-143, www.cpsc.gov/en/Recalls/2012/Todson-Recalls-Bicycle-Child-Carrier-Seats-Due-to-Laceration-and-Fingertip-Amputation-Hazards/.)

that particular style of rack. Note also that the classic seat tube–mounted child seat can often be used on a bike with a rack, as if the rack weren't there.

Lack of suspension could be a serious issue with a rack-mounted seat. Bumps and vibrations are amplified for the child situated over the rear wheel and, in our unscientific opinion, could potentially become dangerous for the child if the system is too rigid. An easy way to provide more suspension for your child is to let a little bit of air out of the back tire. Not so much that you'll pinch the tube or make the bike feel sloppy in turns, but enough to give it a little more bounce and a little less bang. Inexperienced bike owners probably shouldn't mess around with air pressure too much; figure out the basics when you're alone on the bike. In the meantime, use a shop's expertise. We wish we could reach out of this book and check the pressure on your tires from here. (On second thought, maybe not. That could be a pretty creepy superpower.)

A secure harness with rubberized straps is nice to have. Ideally the harness will hold the kid somewhat upright if and when she falls asleep. Kids also appreciate a little soft padding on the straps so they won't abrade their shoulders when the going gets bouncy. If your seat didn't come with straps like that, you can make them softer with bandanas, old baby shirts, or what have you.

If you're going to do a significant amount of riding on that same bike but without the kid, look for a seat with a quick release mechanism that lets you yank the seat off and put it back on in a jiffy. Most seats have this feature; some do not.

You'll see a lot of consistency among the different companies' recommendations on maximum and minimum ages and weights. Age recommendations have everything to do with liability issues, syncing up with AAP guidelines and such, and don't tell us much about the seats themselves. After all, young toddlers come in a wide range of sizes and weights. None of the companies will say that their seats can be used by children younger than 9 months.

You can ignore the maximum age recommendations, but don't second-guess the manufacturers' recommendations on maximum weight. If your toddler is too large for the seat, you can find (with some difficulty perhaps) a rear-mounted seat built for larger kids. The Bobike Junior, for instance, is rated for kids up to 70 pounds. Beyond that, it's time to try one (or more) of the other options: trailers, long bikes, cargo bikes, and the rest.

Product List

Bellelli Pepe. About $125. Maximum capacity: 50 pounds. Weight: 10 pounds. Cutouts in seat for ventilation.

Bobike Maxi. About $200. Maximum capacity: 48 pounds. Made in the Netherlands.

Dieffe GP. About $100. Rack-mounted and seat tube–mounted versions. Maximum capacity: 48.5 pounds. Weight: 9.4 pounds. Italian.

Thule RideAlong. $180. Maximum capacity: 48.5 pounds.
Dimensions: 32 x 18.3 x 18 inches. Weight: 10.2 pounds.

The Thule RideAlong
with padded harness
and seat tube mounting
bracket *Courtesy Thule*

Rear child carriers will change the
feel of any given bike, but you'll get
used to it pretty quick. *Courtesy Thule*

Topeak BabySeat II. About $180. Attaches to a rack that comes
with the seat. Disc brake compatible. Includes crossbar. Maximum
capacity: 40 pounds. Dimensions: 30.5 x 23 x 15.5 inches. Weight:
8 pounds, 2 ounces. Take note of recall notices for previous
versions of this product.

Yepp Maxi. About $230. Maximum
capacity: 48 pounds. Dimensions: 32 x
20 x 15 inches. Weight: 11.75 pounds.
Good adjustability.

Yepp Maxi rear carrier with seat tube
bracket, in an atypical subdued color.
Courtesy Yepp

Trade-Offs

Advantages: Good for bicycle handling and maneuverability; easy to use.

Disadvantages: Putting the child in the seat can be awkward and dangerous without a double kickstand; compatibility issues with some bikes; unlike kids in trailers, passengers in seats go down with the bike in case of a crash.

CHAPTER 8

Trailers

Turn Your Bike into a Semitruck

You can hook up a trailer to just about any bike imaginable. This means that anybody with a working bike can start hauling their kids around for a few hundred bucks. Then, when you're done pulling the trailer, you just unhitch it and you've got your bike back again. The trailer's separability from the bike is a huge advantage.

If you've only got one bike, you won't have to get another one. You're set. In our case, when Bea was old enough, we just started hooking up and unhooking the trailer to the classic steel racing bikes we already owned. Our bikes thus go from utilitarian haulers to performance road bikes and back, and we don't even think twice about it. That's something we wouldn't be comfortable doing with a child seat, cantilevering an extra 50 pounds of bouncing child and chair off the racing bike's thin seat tube. But when the weight's in the trailer and attached to the bike down low, the strain on the bike is limited. We imagine that even a super-light carbon race bike could become a tractor for a kid's trailer, but all the zeros on the bike's price tag would surely make anybody think twice before trying that.

InStep trailers like this one are equipped with smaller wheels and plastic rims, part of what keeps InStep's prices lower than other trailer companies. *Courtesy Thinkstock.com*

The u-joint on the trailer hitch allows the bike to lean without tipping the trailer.
Robert Hurst

The trailer allows for some arrangements that would not be possible with other modes. We bought an extra hitch so we could each have one on our bike 24/7. In the morning one of us (Robert) hauls Bea to preschool and leaves the trailer there, then the other one (Christie) comes along in the afternoon after work and takes the trailer and child back home. Can't do that with a *bakfiets*.

When people list things they dislike about pulling a trailer, they often mention the feel of it. The trailer is a big drag. It's much harder for a cyclist to get through the air while pulling a trailer, and the extra weight and rolling resistance doesn't help either. The more you pull it, the stronger you'll get. No joke. The weight of the trailer also affects the handling of the bike, and you'll feel it pushing on you almost as much as you're pulling on it.

The act of hitching the trailer to the bike can be a little bit fiddly, just enough to mention. With the Burley system, sometimes it takes a minute to get the pin lined up and pushed through. For one parent working alone, it can get tricky to wrangle the kid while hooking up the trailer. And the

Trailers turn any bike, even a fancy road racer, into the family station wagon.
Robert Hurst

more you hurry, of course, the harder it is. With experience trailer users learn tricks to keep the kids occupied while they hook up the trailer.

Nothing is perfect. Certainly not bike trailers.

Roll Over, Roll Over

American conventional wisdom scores safety among the trailer's advantages over child seats, because the child is protected somewhat in that aluminum/ nylon cocoon and won't take a tumble even if mommy or daddy wipes out hard. The American Academy of Pediatrics thinks trailers are preferable to child seats (although they kind of hate them both).[1] There really is very scant evidence to support the claim that trailers are substantially safer than child seats—and few if any have made the claim that trailers are safer than cargo bikes of any kind. But it does seem to make sense to experienced family bikers that trailers would be relatively safe.

One factor that often goes unstated by experienced bikers and overlooked by newcomers is the trailer's propensity to roll over. If one of the trailer's wheels strikes a curb, it will often pop that side of the trailer pretty high into the air (a lot higher than most riders realize until they actually see it happen to somebody else's trailer, or their own trailer rolls because of it.) Combine this with a turn in the wrong direction and that trailer's going over.

It's a lot easier to make a trailer roll than most haulers realize. "I have tipped the trailer more than once by taking a corner too close and having a wheel hit a curb," said Jonathan Maus, founder and editor of BikePortland .com and experienced user of several different kid-hauling modes, when we asked him if he thought child seats were more dangerous than trailers. "Everything we do has some element of danger. . . . But even with three kids and thousands of miles of biking and several spills, we have never had a serious injury. Usually there's no injury at all, except for a few frayed nerves."[2]

These rollovers are traumatic moments for the passenger. But if the harness has been properly secured and the child is wearing a helmet, actual physical injuries should be minimal. If the trailer meets federal standards for the product (as defined by ASTM F 1975-09 5), it should hold up and protect the kid.

Instead of learning all this for yourself, start out with an awareness of the trailer's special weakness. Take great care with the wheels, especially when negotiating curb cuts. The typical trailer is wide enough that you really need to think about what you're doing whenever riding on a sidewalk or path, even if no other bikes or pedestrians are present. Any kind of drop-off or curb at the edge of the sidewalk must be carefully avoided. Don't charge into gaps or hug parked cars.

Really get to know exactly where those wheels track. On the Burley Bee, the left side of the trailer sticks out a few inches farther than the right side. So when we negotiate narrow gaps, we ride the bike a few inches right of center to compensate. When we ride pretty much anywhere with the trailer, come to think of it, we ride a few inches to the right to compensate for that extra trailer width on the left.

Trailers on the Street

The danger of getting smashed by a car is another matter entirely. According to some, parents should not pull their kids in trailers on streets "with traffic." The folks at *Consumer Reports*, for instance, are very serious about mongering trailer-related fear along with their reviews of various models, veering into some extreme advice: "Bike trailers should only be used on trails, never where there is vehicular traffic."[3] Never, they say. Following this advice, of course, would preclude the use of trailers for any actual transportation purpose, even in the most bike path–happy communities in the world. We could go on and on about how absurd this is. It's not just bad advice, it's ridiculous advice. It's unworkable advice, with no basis in reality. Luckily, *Consumer Reports* isn't a go-to authority for family biking pointers. Stick to testing products, folks.

Sadly, the people at *Consumer Reports* could just be following the lead of more authoritative voices. In 1997 the American Academy of Pediatrics recommended that parents not ride bikes with their kids, in trailers or otherwise, on roadways.[4] With plenty of time to rethink, they re-upped this position in 2009: "Bicyclists with young passengers should stick to parks, bike paths and quiet streets to minimize collisions with automobiles."[5]

Digging deeper into the annals of AAP recommendations, however, we can find more carefully thought out guidance: "Preferably ride with passengers in parks, on bike paths, or on quiet streets. Avoid busy thoroughfares and bad weather, and ride with maximum caution and at a reduced speed."[6] When you take out the "should stick to" and replace it with the much softer "preferably," AAP's guidance is similar to the advice we give in this book. When it comes to bikes, the AAP doesn't even want to follow its own best guidance, pushing and pulling at itself.

Sometimes the things you think people *should* do overlap with the things they *can't* do. Like Rock crushes Scissors, Can't destroys Should every time. Parents haul their kids in trailers on suburban and city streets all over the nation. For some it is their only available reliable transportation. More and more families are living car-free, by choice or otherwise, and they can't help noticing that the paths rarely take them where they need to go. They need to ride the streets. That's the reality. Could it really be the conventional wisdom in the boardrooms of law firms and insurance agencies, in police stations and emergency rooms, in the fast-food lines in middle America, that trailers should only be used off-street? Frightening, but that is indeed the belief of many Americans. They see you out there and feel that some sort of violation is being committed.

And do the manufacturers agree that their products shouldn't be used on roadways? Nobody will come out and say it—think of the sales that would be lost. But they don't want to appear to condone street cycling either, in this pathetic CYA world. So they persist in weasel limbo.

Is your child really in more danger of being injured on the street than injured on a bike path, as *Consumer Reports* and the AAP and most of America assume? *Of course!* comes the shouted reply. But bike paths can be plenty dicey too. The likelihood of getting hit by a car on a path may be low, but the likelihood of crashing and being injured could very well be higher. We've certainly had a few close calls with abysmal bike riders on the local paths while pulling our daughter in the trailer. Maybe the American Academy of Pediatrics and *Consumer Reports* should revise their recommendation, from no riding in traffic to no riding at all.

Let's all sit on the couch, all the time. No, we could tumble off the couch and get hurt, so we'd better just sit on the floor. But first, let's all pile into the car and hurtle down the highway at 80 miles per hour to a distant Smashburger.

Parents looking for specific hard numbers or research papers on car-trailer collisions aren't going to find much, if anything. In a way that's really good news. There simply aren't enough incidences of trailer-involved crashes to show up on the statistical radar. (The only known sizable study that looked for trailer-related injuries found that the government agency responsible for monitoring injuries related to every consumer product in the United States didn't have a code for bike trailers.)[7] That doesn't mean that accidents haven't happened. They certainly have, with tragic and horrifying results. We can think of a few terrible stories right now off the top of our heads, and have heard of some lucky escapes too. These stories are in our thoughts whenever we take Bea out in the trailer. But not enough hard data is available to make any grand proclamations about the danger related to other activities or other baby-hauling methods.

The thing that scares people most about trailers is their alleged low profile. Trailers seem like they would be so easy for drivers to overlook. Perhaps that is true. The underlying reality of street riding—any street riding—is the average motorist's persistent failure to notice other road users, especially bicyclists, motorcyclists, and pedestrians. Many of us have seen or been involved in a collision caused by a motorist who failed to notice a large car or huge truck right in front of them. Could a driver overlook your trailer? You bet. Will the orange flag do the trick? Not necessarily.

Just as is the case for a bicyclist traveling alone, it's also difficult for a parent with a passenger in a trailer to pin down exactly which situations present the most danger. The vast majority of reported car-bike collisions involve turning or crossing and occur at some sort of intersection, such as a street, alley, or driveway. However, the most dangerous and deadly collisions are hit-from-behind crashes on roads with higher speed limits. In both cases, seemingly very different, the primary cause of collision is the motorist's failure to notice what's right in front of the vehicle. The general idea for the biker, then, is to minimize your dependence on motorists' and other road users' awareness.

The most effective and easiest tool at the cyclist's disposal is route choice. When hauling your kids (in a trailer or otherwise), be dogged in seeking out the safest, easiest routes (see "Route Choice" on page 35). Find paths and quiet streets, then ride in the middle of them, away from parked cars and driveways. Use empty or sparsely populated sidewalks with discretion and great care (see "Sidewalk Riding" on page 38). If possible avoid high-speed roads and roads with a lot of side traffic.

When sharing streets with motorists traveling the same direction, be courteous and patient—the golden rule of traffic cycling. It's natural to want to carve out as much space as possible and defend it fiercely, especially with a baby on board, mama bear style. But there must be compromise even when hauling kids. Ultimately it's easier that way, for cyclist and driver. Don't ride in the most selfish manner and then expect drivers to treat you with courtesy and respect.

The trailer presents more of a problem for road-sharing and traffic courtesy than other kid-carrying modes. Trailers, in reality, are significantly wider than the bike-and-rider, and, in the imagination of drivers, seem even larger. Trailers are wide enough to really derail the whole system, as many drivers freeze up instead of passing, even when there really is plenty of room. Maybe this could be considered a safety feature, because drivers are more likely to slow and pass carefully. Or maybe that's a stretch. We don't think that drivers who have a hard time passing individual bicyclists will be any better at passing a trailer. We recommend using a mirror when pulling kids in the trailer, whether on the street or a path, to make dealing with faster traffic a little bit easier, but it's not a necessity.

Infants in Trailers

Babies under 1 year can be safely transported in trailers and in *bakfietsen* with the proper precautions (see "Riding with Infants" on page 18). However, not everybody agrees with this.

Many semi-official arbiters of safety, like the American Academy of Pediatrics, can't even seem to comprehend it. They have yet to address the possibility of putting an infant in a car seat and, in turn, securing that car seat in a trailer or cargo box. To them, any baby on a bike needs to wear a helmet, and since kids under 1 year of age supposedly aren't ready for helmets (popping instantaneously into helmet-wearing territory when they turn 1 year old), those kids simply don't ride. It is, of course, arbitrary and simpleminded. You don't put a helmet on your infant when he's in the car seat going down the highway at 80 miles per hour. For infants in trailers and cargo boxes, the car seat itself serves as a sort of full-body helmet, with a roll bar.

You'll notice that the trailer makers sell infant slings and harnesses, even infant carrier-mounting adapters, among their trailer accessories. They would like to capitalize on the growing market for car-free families with new babies. At the same time, they don't want to appear to condone, in writing, the carrying of infants behind bicycles, not with so much pooh-poohing from the AAP, CDC, and CPSC.

So how do manufacturers have their cake and eat it too? Check the fine print. They mention, ever so quietly, that the infant slings and carriers are only to be used when the trailer has been converted to a regular stroller or jogging stroller, or if the child is old enough to wear a helmet.

Buyer's Guide

Trailers come in two general sizes: single, which fits one child comfortably but one child only, and standard/double, which fits two kids a bit like sardines in a can or one kid in relative luxury. The width savings of the single-kid trailer is usually 3 to 5 inches—considerable but nothing to write home about. Trailer width is a critical variable in this mode of travel, so take note of the differences between brands. For instance the two-seat Burleys are about 4 or 5 inches skinnier, wheel-to-wheel, than the two-seat Croozers.

A short list of features should be present on any trailer, for any price. Look for real safety harnesses, of course. Also get a rain cover, rear cargo area (this space is useful but also an important safety feature in case the trailer gets rear-ended), and a lot of reflective material all over the thing. A trailer should also feature a recessed area behind the child's head for a helmet, so his head isn't forced down by the helmet. (Note that the Wike trailers require the purchase of an optional $20 pad [Helmet Relief Pad] to create space behind the passenger's head for the helmet.) It should also have a safety flag.

Bike trailers suitable for hauling children are available at a wide variety of price points, from a few hundred bucks to well over a thousand. The price differences are huge, but the quality differences aren't that obvious.

If you're the type who likes to turn everyday consumer items into status symbols, then the Winther Dolphin is probably what you're looking for. It costs about $1,500, depending on the dollar-Euro exchange rate. You could probably find it on sale somewhere for $1,000 or so. It's a great trailer, made in Denmark. Winther goods are known for attention to detail, such as cantilevered wheels for better handling. Nobody at the playground will have seen that before and will instantly understand—when they see you roll up with your kid riding like some kind of exalted prince—that you mean serious parenting business.

If you just want a decent trailer that won't give you any trouble, they're easy to find. You won't have to order one from Denmark, let's put it that way. Several brands offer fine trailers for about $300. They have all the crucial features listed above, plus things like foldability and quick-release wheels. The Burley Bee is the old standby, and maybe even a standout at this price. The Thule Cadence is similar.

For $70 to $100 more, these brands will sell you a trailer that converts to a stroller, giving you more versatility (and about 7 to 10 pounds in additional weight if the stroller wheel and bar must be carried). Jury's out on whether or not that's worth it (see "Convertible Child Carriers" on page 94).

Subtle yet important improvements lead to the next price point. Zippers! Zippers are cool, actually. Sometimes the Bee's zipperless, snapless cover comes loose, believe it or not. (The covers of cheaper trailers

Burley will sell you an infant carrier like this for use in their trailers, but won't officially condone carrying unhelmeted infants. *Courtesy Burley*

rely on elastic and Velcro to stay in place.) Quite often we find ourselves stopping to reattach it so it's not draped over our daughter's helmet. A zipper would be nice, we think to ourselves every time.

More expensive trailers also have better harnesses. Above $400 or so you start to find nice, padded shoulder straps, whereas the Bee and similar trailers have plain webbing straps. Unpadded straps can be a problem if they're rubbing on the kid's exposed skin. In a crash the padded straps would likely perform a lot better as well. You can fix unpadded straps by fashioning your own pads or simply by buying some.

One feature we like to find on trailers, but usually don't until the price is over $400, is a sunshade. Sitting strapped into the trailer, your kid is often at the mercy of the sun for long periods of time. Even through the standard screen the sun can get very oppressive and even dangerous for the child. We fashioned our own crude sunshade for the Bee, but it sure would be nice to have a dedicated, easy-to-use shade.

Climb a little higher still, over $500, and the trailers have suspension, which is very cool. Suspension is not going to eliminate vibration or any potential hazard associated with vibration, but it will definitely help. We're not sure, but suspension seems like a positive for safety as well, perhaps making the trailer less likely to overturn when one wheel strikes a curb or some other object. Croozer Plus trailers have "self-adjusting" elastomer suspension, while the top-end Burleys have adjustable suspension.

Among the budget options, InStep is a popular brand. These trailers will do the job most of the time. For $200 or less you can get a basic trailer that will convert to a stroller. Take note of the weight, however. Their double-seat Rocket II model weighs 10-plus pounds more than the Burley Bee, and the cargo capacity is lower. Note as well the wheels, which on the low-end InSteps have smaller 16-inch tires on molded plastic rims. Expect those smaller, low-quality wheels to affect ride quality. All the other trailers listed below have 20-inch spoked wheels.

Also, InStep's low-end trailers—and all of Wike's trailers—are without wheel guards, which doesn't seem like a good idea to us. It's not difficult to think up scenarios in which wheel guards would save you and your child from injury. Somewhat reluctantly, we added these trailers to the list anyway.

Convertible Child Carriers

We've already mentioned trailers that can be converted to strollers. Another version is the stroller that can be converted to a trailer. (It could be a distinction made more by marketing departments than reality.) It's fundamentally the same thing—a big trailer-looking object with an aluminum frame and nylon cover—except with the so-called convertible child carrier, you have to pay extra to get the bike trailer conversion hardware.

If you're wondering whatever became of the popular and expensive Chariot trailers, the company was purchased by Thule, which turned all the Chariot models into Thule Chariot Convertible Child Carriers. Since they are now sold as strollers first and trailers second, we left them off the list. Check them out if you like well-designed products and can afford the premium prices. Then don't forget to add another $80 or so for the bike trailer conversion kit, which is not included.

You should ask yourself, before buying any sort of trailer/stroller/jogging stroller transformer, if you really want to use a stroller that is—let's face it—not really a stroller at all. It's clearly a bike trailer. Even the convertible child carriers aren't fooling anybody. Putting a handle on the back and a wheel or two on the front doesn't suddenly change it into something other than a bike trailer.

Using a bike trailer as a stroller does work, and a lot of parents take advantage of this and never get another stroller. Many parents who own convertible trailers, however, only use it as a stroller on rare occasions, finding their trailer-turned-stroller to be too darn big and trailer-like for the job at hand. They get a dedicated stroller or two anyway.

Convertible trailers make a lot more sense to parents who want a jogging stroller with the necessary big wheels, those who have two kids to wrangle, or those who need a carrier when they get to their destination on the bike. It's a lot easier to convert the trailer than to carry a stroller around in the back of the trailer.

Convertible trailers have parking brakes and, often, handlebars that fold down. The bars are meant to stay on in trailer mode. This adds to the weight of the trailer but also gives it a more effective roll bar, supposedly. We're not sure how much safer this would be for your passengers.

Product List

Burley Bee. $299. Seats one or two. Does not convert to stroller. At 18 pounds, one of the lighter trailers available. Width: 30 inches.

Burley Cub. $629. Seats one or two. Hard-bottomed, all-terrain model. Includes sunshade, padded harnesses, zippered rain cover, and adjustable suspension. Convertible to stroller. Stroller kits sold separately. Almost 20 pounds heavier than the Bee, according to

Burley's website (www.burley.com/page_307/cub.html). Width: 30 inches.

Burley D'Lite. $629. Top-of-the-line model offers everything that comes with the Encore, plus adjustable suspension. Convertible to stroller. Stroller kits sold separately. Width: 31 inches.

Burley Encore. $449. The mid-grade model, with sunshade and padded harness, zippered rain cover, and more. Convertible to stroller. Stroller kits sold separately. Width: 31 inches.

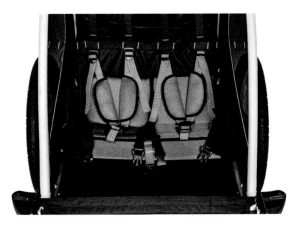

The Burley Encore comes with slightly upgraded harnesses and seats.
Courtesy Burley

Burley Honey Bee. $399. Seats one or two. Like the Bee but convertible to a stroller. Includes stroller kit. Width: 30 inches.

Convertible trailers, like this Burley Honey Bee, are more expensive and a little heavier too.
Courtesy Burley

Burley Solo. $529. Seats one. The one-seat version of the D'Lite. Adjustable suspension. Convertible to stroller. Stroller kits sold separately. Width: 27.5 inches.

Croozer Kid Plus. $475. Seats one. Converts to stroller. Includes stroller kit. Suspension. Width: 31 inches.

Croozer Kid Plus For 2. $675. Seats one or two. Converts to stroller. Includes stroller kit. Suspension. Width: 35 inches.

InStep Quick N EZ Double. $170. Seats one or two. Includes stroller kit. 16-inch molded plastic rims. Width: 33 inches

InStep Rocket II. $250. Seats one or two. Includes stroller kit. Spoked wheels. Width: 35 inches.

InStep Sync. $130. Seats one. Convertible to stroller. Does not include stroller kit. 16-inch molded plastic rims. Width: 26 inches. *Note:* Maximum weight limit for this trailer is a mere 40 pounds.

Thule Cadence. $299. Seats one or two. Does not convert to stroller. Width: 31.5 inches.

The Thule Cadence
Courtesy Thule

TRAILER RECALLS

- A recall on products made in Chariot's Canadian facility from December 2005 to June 2010, prior to its acquisition by Thule. No injuries were reported in twenty-four failed hitch incidents. Chariot provided its customers with replacement hitches that the customers were supposed to install themselves. ("Chariot Carriers Recalls Child Bicycle Trailers and Conversion Kits Due to Injury Hazard," US Consumer Product Safety Commission, January 11, 2012, Release #12-085, www.cpsc.gov/en/Recalls/2012/Chariot-Carriers-Recalls-Child-Bicycle-Trailers-and-Conversion-Kits-Due-to-Injury-Hazard/.)

- Affecting some Burley D'Lite ST and Solo ST models—the good stuff—manufactured in the Philippines in 2008. The company determined that the axle sleeves could loosen and allow a wheel to fall off. Not only were no injuries reported for this one, but no incidents were reported. Burley offered customers repair kits and free help with the repairs if desired. ("Burley Design Recalls Child Trailers Due to Risk of Injury," CPSC, August 19, 2009, Release #09-310, www.cpsc.gov/en/Recalls/2009/Burley-Design-Recalls-Child-Trailers-Due-to-Risk-of-Injury/.)

Order extra hitches if you want to set up multiple bikes to pull the trailer. *Courtesy Burley*

Thule Coaster. $379. Seats one or two. Convertible to stroller. Stroller kit included. Width: 31.5 inches.

Wike Premium Double. $470, including Helmet Relief Pad. Seats one. Padded harness. Convertible to stroller. Stroller kits not included. Width: 32 inches.

Wike Premium Single. $470, including Helmet Relief Pad. Seats one. Padded harness. Convertible to stroller. Stroller kits not included. Width: 28 inches.

Wike Softie. $620, including Helmet Relief Pad. Seats one or two. Elastomer suspension. Padded harness. Convertible to stroller. Stroller kits not included. Width: 32 inches.

Wike XP. $295, including Helmet Relief Pad. Seats one or two. Not convertible to stroller. Width: 30 inches.

Winther Dolphin NE. €1,000! Convertible to "push-buggy." Made in Denmark. High quality, highest price.

Trade-Offs

Advantages: More affordable than a cargo bike; safety in minor crashes; cargo-carrying capability (can carry two kids); can accommodate a wide range of ages and sizes; infant-carrying capability with special carrier; separability means you can use the same bike for recreation or other purposes.

Disadvantages: Width and length; susceptible to rollovers; potential visibility issues in traffic; somewhat unwieldy.

CHAPTER 9

Front-Loading Cargo Bikes

Bakfiets Means "Greatest Thing Ever" in Danish

The traditional front-loading cargo bike, commonly called a *bakfiets* ("box bike"), is a weird-looking contraption to American eyes. It's like half bike, half wheelbarrow. The main idea behind the bakfiets (plural is *bakfietsen*) is to combine the cargo-carrying capacity of a big cargo trike, which in Europe is also called a bakfiets, with the far superior handling characteristics of a two-wheeler.

These machines are traditionally set up with a 26-inch wheel in back and a little 20-inch wheel up front—way, way up front. The front wheel is connected to the handlebars with a long steering arm attached to its front fork. Between the front wheel and the rider is a sizable cargo box, traditionally made of marine plywood. It's so Euro.

Riding a front-loading two-wheeler is a little funky at first, but anybody who can ride a bike can learn within minutes. Of course you'll want to acquaint yourself with the handling characteristics before trying to ride with kid(s) on board. (Riding no hands is pretty much impossible, so don't try.) But the general consensus is that riding bakfietsen is surprisingly easy.

The Bullitt is a relatively racy machine that combines the traditional "Long John" design with a lighter frame and more aggressive geometry. *Courtesy Bullit*

As noted earlier in the book, if you want—or need—to transport an infant by bicycle, one of the best ways to do it is to put her in a protective car seat or carrier that is then latched down securely in the box of a traditional bakfiets. Some companies really have this down, providing special frame-works and latches for this purpose. The old-school, high-quality cargo bike companies like WorkCycles will set you up with everything you need to haul babies the right way. Know that the American Academy of Pediatrics doesn't think you should try to carry a kid by bike until she turns 1 year old, although they don't offer consistent reasoning for their recommendation (see "How Young Is Too Young?" on page 15).

Talk to your pediatrician about it first. If you decide to carry your baby like this, try to somehow soften the vibrations and jarring that can occur, not only by riding very gingerly but also by placing a pillow or folded-up blanket in the box under the car seat. Note that carrying a car seat in the box makes it difficult, although not impossible, to carry a few spare toddlers in it as well.

Many experienced family bikers think the front-loading cargo bike is the ultimate tool for transporting kids. Its advantages are many. First of all, it's really nice to have your kids right there in front of you. You can interact with them and see everything they're up to. The thing is also surprisingly stable and maneuverable.

If you do crash a bakfiets, it won't be as dangerous for the passengers—more like tipping over, because you probably won't be going very fast. Com-bined with a good bench and harness, machines of this sort provide decent protection for passengers in case of the rare crash or low-speed collision. (A high-speed collision is another matter, but then, that's the case with virtually all modes of transportation.) In all seriousness, the anchor-like properties of these big rigs keep the occupants safer. If you can get one going more than 20 miles per hour on flat ground, more power to you!

The disadvantages are well known too. The aforementioned heavyweight reality of the bakfiets isn't such a bad thing on the streets, until you run into a hill. Seventy pounds or more is typical for a steel rig. Those who use big cargo bikes in hilly cities are fueling a fast-expanding business: electronic assist motors (see "Electric Assist" on page 132).

The bakfiets remains a real chunk even when you're not riding it. If you have to carry the thing around at all it's an ordeal. Taking it up and down stairs is more of a two-person job. Just finding a place to store such a large object can be difficult. With the box on, it can be very tough to get through doorways. Families who live in upstairs apartments might have to ditch the whole cargo bike idea, unless some kind of special arrangement can be made. (Due to the behemoth qualities of bakfietsen, they really are designed to be stored outdoors.) Putting a cargo bike in a car or train—trying to go multi-modal with it in any way—is going to be darn near impossible.

Because of the bakfiets's somewhat unique mechanical setup and pervasive Euro-ness, it could develop some issues that stymie the kids at the local bike shop in Akron or Denver. The farther away you get from Northern Europe (we'll include Portland, Oregon, in that geography), the less likely it is that anybody even knows what bakfietsen are.

With a price tag about 10 to 20 times higher than a trailer's, the traditional cargo bike is among the most expensive kid-carrying options. We think that's their biggest disadvantage. Even the knock-offs are expensive. Can't help noticing that a good-quality box bike costs about the same as a decent used car. It would, however, be a lot cheaper than a car to run and insure.

That's if you can get one. Good luck with that, sincerely.

Buyer's Guide

The level of hassle and difficulty you will experience in trying to purchase a bakfiets for your family depends a great deal on where you live. In our city, getting our hands on a traditional cargo bike is hardly straightforward. Even if we had the money, we'd probably need to have the bike, at least the frame, shipped in. Also, test-riding bikes prior to purchase would be very difficult. There's no trace of a market for used bakfietsen here either, or we'd be all over that. In fact, it's almost impossible to find a used cargo bike for sale in the United States outside of the Pacific Northwest or hipster Brooklyn. That should change soon as more Americans buy more new bakfietsen that then trickle into the used market.

Many of these cargo bike companies are very small operations. CETMA, for instance, consists of one person, Lane Kagay, working in Venice, California. Many of these operations are not only small but located overseas in the homeland of cargo bikes. The "boutique" nature of the cargo bike biz—or so it looks to us in the United States—has some important consequences for potential customers. On the one hand, you can get personal service from the manufacturer, feel good about giving your money to real craftspeople instead of a faceless corporation, and know that the finished product will probably be high quality. On the other hand, the rig's going to cost mega-bucks, and it could take you a long time to get it.

Bakfiets frames can be purchased separately as well, but this is not likely to be a money-saving option unless you already possess many of the needed components, or can get reliable used parts. In general, purchasing components piecemeal will add to the total price tag. Shipping costs are usually the same for frames and complete cargo bikes, so no advantage there.

Front-loading two-wheelers like those listed below can also be combined with racks and/or rear seats to transport multiple children or lots of cargo (although the standard cargo box can carry two kids comfortably along with plenty of other stuff like groceries). Some of these bike makers include a rear cargo rack in their standard package, and others will weld one onto the back of the frame for a few hundred dollars. How about slapping a trailer on that thing too? Well, it's been done, but we don't recommend it. Too long.

Just about any complete front-loading cargo bike comes standard with fenders, a heavy-duty kickstand, and lights powered by hub dynamos, which is great. The quality of the components does vary a fair bit though, so be aware. The Dutch love chain cases and chain guards, because they allow pedalers to wear pretty much whatever they want without worrying about deadly chain smudge. Most bakfietsen come with a rear wheel lock—you can just lock the wheel and leave it (for a while anyway) without worrying about any single individual walking away with the bike, unless that person happens to be The Hulk. Just about any bakfiets can be accessorized with a full rain canopy or a flat box cover, but they tend not to be included among standard equipment and are expensive add-ons. One bakfiets rain canopy will cost about as much as a decent trailer.

Almost all of these cargo bike makers will outfit your rig with an electric assist motor on request. It's a nice option in hilly areas. Nice, even considered necessary by some, but generally quite expensive. Several different types of e-assist motors are available, with some variation in price and quality (see "Electric Assist" on page 132).

Don't worry too much about picking a frame size. These bikes are usually one-size-fits-all, or rather one-size-fits-most, with adjustable seat and handlebar height and that's it. That's the way it goes with European utility bikes. Parents who are either very small or tall could have difficulty making a bakfiets work. Unfortunately it will be difficult to road test different models to compare their fit and feel. It doesn't help that people who have used many different types of bakfietsen report obvious differences in handling from bike to bike.

In addition to these traditional cargo haulers that place the load down low, behind the front wheel, there are front-loaders that have their cargo boxes above the front wheel. (The cargo bike by Bilenky Cycle Works is a well-known example.) These are much better suited to hauling boxes and other cargo than children.

Some of the makers of traditional cargo bikes offer a "sportier" version that has a shorter box and shorter wheelbase than the standard bakfiets. These have less cargo capacity but still do a great job of hauling a single kid. Prices, unfortunately, tend to be about the same.

Speaking of prices, notice that some of the prices below are listed in Euros. So for a customer in the United States, the price changes on a constant basis with the exchange rate. With few US dealers setting solid dollar prices on these things, it makes more sense to print the European price. Just keep in mind that the actual cost to a customer in the United States can vary quite widely from week to week based on political and economic circumstances. When we wrote this, the exchange rate was 1.2 dollars to the Euro.

As always, keep in mind that any prices you see in this book are subject to change, and change quickly they will. Almost always the change is in an upward direction.

Product List

Babboe City. $2,150. Includes birch cargo box, bench and two seat belts, cargo kickstand, fenders, and lights. Steel frame. Internally

geared hub (Shimano Nexus 7-speed). Roller brakes front and rear (Shimano). Length: 255 centimeters (8.4 feet). Box has step-ups to make it easier for kids to get in. Dutch bike, China built.

The Babboe City comes with a stylish, corner-less cargo box. *Courtesy Babboe*

Bakfiets.nl CargoBike Long. €1,609–1,759, depending on number of speeds (3–8) and type of brake (roller brake or coaster brake). Internally geared hub (Shimano Nexus). Electric model also available. Steel frame. Made in Holland. This is the classic design, and one of the most basic bakfietsen available.

Bakfiets.nl CargoBike Short. €1,559–1,709, depending on number of speeds (3–8) and type of brake (roller brake or coaster brake). Internally geared hub (Shimano Nexus). Electric model also available. Steel frame. Made in Holland.

Some cargo bike companies offer a smaller version of the traditional *bakfiets*, like this Bakfiets.nl. *Courtesy Bakfiets.nl*

Bakfiets.nl CargoBike Premium. €1,939–1,999, depending on number of speeds (7–8). Comes with an assortment of upgrades. Internally geared hub (Shimano Nexus). Electric model also available. Steel frame. Made in Holland. A fancier version of the classic bakfiets.

CETMA Margo (Mini). $3,500 with uncoated wooden box. External gearing (SRAM X-7 10-speed). NuVinci continuously variable transmission hub available. Disc brakes (Avid BB7).

Bike can be separated into two pieces. Wheelbase: 76 inches. "CETMA cargo bikes are handmade by one guy near the beach in Los Angeles." Also available with larger cargo areas (the Largo and Hugo models).

You could carry some seriously heavy children around in these CETMA cargo bikes, handmade in Venice Beach. *Courtesy CETMA*

Eendraght Milano. $2,250. Includes box, bench, and safety harnesses. Battery lighting. Roller brakes. Internally geared hub (Shimano Nexus). Steel frame. Black only. This is a classic-looking bakfiets that matches the dimensions of the Bakfiets.nl CargoBike Long.

Frances Cycles Small Haul. $3,000, frame only. Includes canvas cargo bag and two headsets. (Complete bikes can be ordered: "Call for details.") 80-pound cargo capacity. A lighter front-loader with a unique style and soft bag. People do use them to carry kids, but it's a different sort of situation. Custom-built in Santa Cruz, California. francescycles.com.

Gazelle Cabby. $2,500–$3,000. Includes collapsible soft-sided box, bench and safety harnesses, chain case, and rack. Unique steel frame. Roller brakes. Internally geared hub (Shimano Nexus 7-speed). Weight: 85 pounds. Dutch design, factory made in China. One reviewer found the Gazelle's roller brakes to be inadequate for hilly terrain.[1] US dealers somewhat hard to find.

Human Powered Machines Long Haul. $3,050, with wooden box, internal hub gearing (SRAM), and disc brakes (Avid BB7). Also available with rim brakes and derailleur gearing. Rack mounts and fenders extra. Steel frame. Wheelbase: 73 inches. Made in Eugene, Oregon.

JoeBike ShuttleBug. $6,000–$8,000 (!), depending on components. Includes steel-framed canvas cargo carrier. Steel frame. Made in Portland, Oregon. The ShuttleBug was a relatively light bakfiets with geometry and components spec'd for Portland's hilly terrain. Unfortunately the cost was astronomical and waiting lists were long. This was too much success for JoeBike. They pulled the plug on the Bug! This bit from their website illustrates the funkiness of the bakfiets industry: "After much deliberation, we've decided not to make more of these [ShuttleBugs]. We are a small and relatively new retail shop that got into the framebuilding business because nobody was making the bike we knew could be made. While the bike was a big success critically and commercially, with orders booked up for several months for many more bikes than we were physically capable of making (even at a price point of $8,000 or more), framebuilding was a whole separate enterprise, industry, physical site, and business. Only the staff—our framebuilders also worked as expert mechanics at our retail shop, a decision that proved invaluable to the design of the bike—were the same. On that note, we are interested in selling our proprietary designs, including the drawings, exact tubing specifications, the FEA report, the ShuttleBug name, and any other intellectual property associated with the ShuttleBug. Our goals are to put this bike back into the world, serving families and others, and to save the manufacturer a good deal of time and money versus the time and money needed to design, test, and develop a bike of this kind organically. Contact us if you're an interested manufacturer or framebuilder."[2]

Larry vs Harry Bullitt. About €1,800–3,200 plus shipping, depending on component package. Some distributors in the United States. Internally geared hub or external gearing available. Aluminum frame. Bike length (front tire edge to back tire edge): 243 centimeters (8 feet). Made in Denmark. An industry-oriented cargo bike that has taken the family biking world by storm. Lighter and much more aggressively angled than traditional bakfietsen. (http://larryvsharry.com.)

Hot pink Bullitt. Various cargo box variations are available at additional cost. *Courtesy Bullitt*

This yellow Bullitt is equipped with a BionX pedal assist system, to really get things moving (see "Electric Assist"). *Courtesy Bullitt*

Metrofiets Standard 8. Approximately $4,500 plus shipping. Includes wooden box, bench seat, and seat belts. Steel frame. Internally geared hub (Shimano Alfine 8-speed). Disc brakes (Avid BB7 Mechanical). Currently, a customer is asked to make a 50 percent down payment to get his name on the list, then the bike is created in the following months. www.metrofiets.com.

Metrofiets Standard 10. Approximately $4,500 plus shipping. Includes wooden box, bench seat, and seat belts. Steel frame. External gearing (Shimano SLX 10-speed). Disc brakes (Avid BB7 Mechanical). www.metrofiets.com.

Made in the USA: The Metrofiets cargo bike is handmade in Portland, Oregon. *Courtesy Metrofiets*

Urban Arrow Family. $5,000-plus. Includes Bosch electric assist and high-density foam box. (Not available without e-assist.) Aluminum frame. NuVinci continuously variable transmission hub. Roller brakes (disc brakes optional). This is the Mercedes 500SL of cargo bikes.

The Urban Arrow is an e-assist bakfiets aimed at urbanites whose income arrow points up. *Courtesy Urban Arrow*

Virtue Gondoliere. $1,500, with wooden cargo box. Steel frame. External gearing (Shimano Acera 7-speed). Drum brake on front wheel (Joytech). Roller brake on rear wheel (Shimano BR-IM31-R). Weight: 28 kilograms (62 pounds). Length: 7.6 feet. Relatively low-priced, but cargo box capacity is only 66 pounds and overall quality is suspect. "I have a hard time imagining how they are selling them for that little. . . .," says Walt Wehner, maker of Waltworks Custom Bicycles.[3]

Winther Wallaroo. Expensive. Includes fully enclosed nylon passenger compartment. Aluminum frame. "Gear hub with footbrake."[4] We suppose that means a coaster brake, which is interesting for such an expensive machine. Disc brake on front wheel. Weight: 33.5 kilograms (74 pounds). Danish design. Not much information available on this one.

WorkCycles Kr8. €1,776 plus shipping. Includes wooden box, bench, and two harnesses. Steel frame. Roller brakes (Shimano IM-80) and internally geared hub (Shimano 8-speed). Chain case and rear cargo rack. Bike can be separated into two pieces. Made in Amsterdam. An improved version of the Bakfiets.nl CargoBike Long, according to WorkCycles.

DIY

Frustrated by the shockingly high prices, long wait times, and lack of availability in the bakfiets market? Make your own! Okay, much easier said than done, but certainly in the realm of the possible. If you're not up for welding, you could always try to make your own cargo box. Check out these online resources for inspiration, ideas, and instructions:

http://felixcollins.blogspot.com/2012/01/homebuilt-bakfiets
 -cargo-bike.html

http://karlonsea.wordpress.com/2012/02/19/frankenbike-progress
 -building-the-box/

http://tomscargobikes.com/tomscargobikes.com/Home.html

www.wired.com/2010/12/diy-cargo-bike-mods/#slideid-442768

Trade-Offs

Advantages: Easy to use; stability under load; two wheels good for handling; allows parent to see and communicate with child.

Disadvantages: Expensive and hard to find; big and heavy; hard to store; can't transport on bus or train.

CHAPTER 10

Cargo Trikes

From Denmark with Love

Front-loading cargo tricycles, ubiquitous in Northern Europe but virtually absent from the United States, are the truckiest of all kid-carrying bikes. These are serious transportation vehicles. Tricycles with two wheels in front and single wheel in back, like those in this section, are known in some circles as "tadpole trikes," which might give you the wrong idea about how substantial some of these things really are.

One big advantage of the three-wheeler is its all-season stability. Ice on the roads and path? Slippery gravel in the turns? The trike stays upright (it may not turn very well, but at least it won't fall over). Its 24/7 stability should not be discounted. The rider's handling prowess, or lack thereof, is removed from the equation. When your two-wheeled comrades are wiping out on sandy roads and longitudinal cracks, you and your kids will be sitting pretty.

The trike's cargo capacity is also exceptional, making it a tempting option for multi-kid families, or those who want to replace the Toyota without having to borrow someone else's truck every time they have to go to the grocery store or Home Depot.

Cargo trikes like this Christiania provide the most stable and carefree family biking option. Also the slowest. *Courtesy Christiania*

Christiania trikes, handmade in Denmark, are equipped with a lawnmower-style handlebar. *Courtesy Christiania*

On the other hand, it's slooow. In fact, the unassisted trike has to be the slowest of all available kid-carrying machines. Commuters notice that their transits take much longer on the trike. Like 50 percent longer, according to one trike family. In other words, it turns a 10-minute ride into a 15-minute ride, a 30-minute ride into a 45-minute ride, and so on. Time is really important in kid-hauling, so the trike's speedlessness is potentially a big negative.

The front-loading cargo trike also shares all the secondary disadvantages of the two-wheeled *bakfiets*: It is extra costly, hard to store, and somewhat hard to purchase. Perhaps the biggest disadvantage of any trike is that it's *not a bike*. Much of the bike's magic has been sucked out, simply by adding that third wheel.

People who have used cargo trikes for a long time have figured out some things that will come as news to the rest of us. "The trike eats saddles," says Patrick Barber, an experienced kid-hauler with a Christiania trike. "Because of the camber of our streets, and the twisting and leaning required to manage turns at speed, we go through a B67 once every two or three years." That's something we never would have thought about, but it makes perfect sense. Patrick figures the problem may have been exacerbated by improper saddle tension.

Despite its quirks and weird flaws, Patrick isn't planning on ditching the family Christiania any time soon. "I'm the kind of guy who likes a nice stable heavy bike with fat tires, and the trike takes that to another level . . . The single, large cargo area provides space and stability to carry, say, a tippy houseplant, or a pizza, or a few kids . . . You don't have to work hard to keep it upright at slow speeds. Quite the opposite. You can pedal as slowly as possible up a hill while drinking a cup of coffee with one hand."[1]

Buyer's Guide

As with two-wheeled *bakfietsen*, high-quality cargo trikes are made by a number of small builders in Europe and North America. The market is also populated by lower-quality offerings factory made in China and assembled elsewhere by distributors trying to capitalize on the decades of customer satisfaction that the respected makers have delivered. It can be difficult to tell which is which sometimes. Sometimes the difference between the copy and the "real thing" is not so great; other times it is.

THE STORY OF CHRISTIANIA

Christiania, a unique Danish town known for its self-government and commitment to environmentalism, was born in 1971 when a group of counterculture squatters took over an abandoned military base in Copenhagen. For a few years Danish authorities tried to expel them from the base, then more or less gave up. Every few years for decades, hard-liners gained control of government posts and dredged up the idea of eradicating Christiania, or at least curtailing its open hash trade—to no avail. Christiania has since gained a great deal of official acceptance and now has an air of permanence about it.

Despite its many external enemies, Christiania's toughest fight may have been an internal struggle. In the late 1970s heroin hit Copenhagen hard. Christiania struggled enough with its heroin issue that its residents eventually tried to team up with the police to bust the dealers. In 1979, according to the *Christiania Guide*, when the police raided the hash dealers instead, Christianites acted on their own. Junkies were allowed to stay, but only if they kicked the habit. Dealers were removed by force. "No hard drugs" remains one of the town's only rules. Other rules include no weapons, no violence, recycle everything that can be recycled, and, of course, no "rocker badges" (*Christiania Guide*, pp. 5, 2, www.christiania.org/wp-content/uploads/2013/02/Guideeng2.pdf).

While the residents' commitment to freedom and hash-smoking gets all the press, the town's real defining feature could be its lack of cars. There is no motor traffic in Christiania. The roads are open for pedestrians to wander as they please. Bicyclists are

This category is dominated (at least psychologically) by Christiania in Denmark, with its iconic hand-built trikes and unique history. Note that the Christiania trikes use a sort of lawnmoweresque handlebar, whereas many of the other trikes use regular handlebars. "We welded (had a friend weld) a pair of Dutch city bike bars onto the existing 'shopping cart handle' and it improved the trike's ride and feel very, very much," says Patrick Barber. The Christianias also aren't equipped with dynamo hubs, which can lead to a lot of nighttime light-wrangling and charging. If you're mega-interested in allowed to go anywhere "at any time with due consideration for pedestrians" (ibid). This created the perfect environment for the development of the Christiania cargo trike, a vehicle that acts like it never needs to hurry.

At first, Christianites made heavy-duty trailers out of old bed frames. Those worked well, but there was room for improvement. The first Christiania cargo trike was made in 1984. Within a few years demand for these super-practical, smog-free vehicles was coming from outside the town and even outside of Denmark. In 1990 production moved out of the Christiania blacksmith shop to the island of Bornholm.

Today the little factory employs fifteen workers. They're quick to point out that the machine has been improved over the decades—refined—but it's still the same basic trike from the old days. If it ain't broke, don't mess with it. The Christiania trike won the Danish Design Award in 2010–2011 and is ubiquitous in the world's two top bike cities, Copenhagen and Amsterdam. (Information from the company's website: http://christianiabikes.com/en/about-cb/history/ and http://christianiabikes.com/en/about-cb/dansk-design/.)

Although Christiania has had periods of trouble—most of it from outside—more than forty years after its anarchist birth, Freetown Christiania is chugging along like the classic cargo trike that bears its name. Though home to only a thousand people or so, it's an increasingly popular place to visit. Tourists flock there to see "something Danish that cannot be found anywhere else in the world" (*Christiania Guide English*, www.christiania.org/info/christiania-guide-english/).

getting a real Christiania trike, check their website for the available iterations. There's a surprising amount of variety in their lineup.

Some of the models listed below are basically knock-offs of Christiania's. There are some other worthy old-school machines, however, and other interesting and fun options. Take a look at the Nihola, for instance, which uses a different, some would say superior, steering system in which the wheels turn independently of the cargo box. Like the Christianias, Nihola trikes are popular in Copenhagen.

Most of the cargo trikes available come with an internally geared hub, usually Shimano Nexus. The brake setups vary a lot from model to model. In general the makers don't get very excited about putting really powerful brakes on cargo trikes, because they don't envision them going fast downhill, or in any other direction. Almost all the models come with some sort of parking brake—think of it as the trike's kickstand.

Electric motors are increasingly common on cargo trikes, as with other forms of cargo bike. Almost all of the trikes below can be ordered from the manufacturer with an electric motor installed. Expect to pay a few extra thousand dollars for that. The UK's VeloElectrique doesn't offer a non-electric trike.

In such a rarified retail environment as this, the prices below should be viewed as approximations. If you see Euros listed instead of dollars, it means we couldn't find a dealer in the United States. That doesn't mean you can't get the machine, but it does mean it will be very difficult, maybe impossible, to try it before buying. The Euro-dollar exchange rate was about 1.2 dollars per Euro when we wrote this, but that's subject to rapid change.

Product List

Babboe Big. $2,499, includes two foldable bench seats and four seat belts, fenders, lights, rear rack, and steering damper.[2] Steel frame. Internally geared hub (Sturmey Archer 5-speed). Drum brakes front and rear (unspecified). Length: 217 centimeters (7.1 feet). 20-inch front wheels, 26-inch rear.

A large cargo box like the one on this Babboe Big model trike will hold up to four kids, or two kids plus cargo. *Courtesy Babboe*

Bakfiets.nl Cargo Trike Large. €1,989, not including shipping. Includes wooden cargo box, two foldable bench seats and four seat belts, generator hub, fenders, and rear rack. Aluminum frame. Internally geared hub (Shimano 7-speed). Roller brake (Shimano). Dutch-made. Available with different brake and hub configurations. Currently there are no dealers for this company located in North America, but they'd love to take your order (http://bakfiets.nl/eng/modellen/cargotrike/large/).

Trikes don't need kickstands but most have parking brakes, useful for loading kids and cargo. Two little girls, a floppy dog, and some mums about to go for a ride in this Bakfiets.nl trike. *Courtesy Bakfiets.nl*

Bakfiets.nl Cargo Trike Small. €1,939, not including shipping. Includes wooden cargo box, foldable bench seat and two seat belts, generator hub, fenders, and rear rack. Aluminum frame. Internally geared hub (Shimano 7-speed). Roller brake (Shimano). Dutch-made. Available with different brake and hub configurations. Currently there are no dealers for this company located in North America, but they'd love to take your order (http://bakfiets.nl/eng/modellen/cargotrike/small/).

Christiania Light. $2,850 with wooden cargo box; bench and seat belts are extra. Aluminum frame. Mechanical disc brakes on front wheels. Maximum load: 100 kilograms (220 pounds) plus driver. Length: 208 centimeters (6.8 feet). Width: 87 centimeters (2.8 feet). Weight: 35 kilograms (77 pounds). Cargo box dimensions: 88 x 62 x 50/36 centimeters (35 x 24 x 20/14 inches) (the standard box slopes downward from back to front). Electric motor available. 24-inch wheels.

Nihola Family. $3,599, includes steel and plastic powdercoated box, bench and two seat belts, and rain hood. Steel frame. Hydraulic steering damper. Available with rear coaster brake (SRAM 5-speed) and front roller brake or freewheel hub (Shimano Nexus 8-speed), V-brake and front roller brake. Length: 2 meters (6.5 feet). Weight: 32 kilograms (70.5 pounds). Cargo box dimensions: 88 (max) x 62 (max) x 50 centimeters (35 x 24 x 20 inches) (box is oblong shaped). Handmade in Denmark.

The Nihola trike from above. Can a cargo trike be "sleek?"
Courtesy Nihola

VeloElectrique Velo Cargo E250. £1,455, includes two removable bench seats, four seat belts, and removable rain cover. Aluminum frame. Electric motor (it's not available without it). Derailleur gears (6-speed Shimano). V-brakes on front wheels and disc brake on rear wheel.

Virtue Schoolbus. $1,000, with wooden cargo box. Steel frame. Derailleur gears (Shimano Acera). V-brake on rear wheel (Promax). Drum brake on front wheel (Sturmey Archer). Weight: 57 pounds. Length: 84 inches. Cargo box dimensions: 37 x 23 x 21 inches. Electric model also available. California company, Chinese trike.

Winther Kangaroo Luxe. $4,499, with enclosed nylon passenger area. Aluminum frame. Front wheel suspension. Adjustable steering damper. Weight: 44 kilograms (97 pounds). Length: 218 centimeters (7.1 feet). Width: 90 centimeters (35 inches). 20-inch front wheels. Internally geared hub (Nexus or SRAM). Hydraulic disc brake on front wheel (Tektro), coaster brake on rear. A very expensive rig with some interesting features. As we wrote this, the only known US distributor was in Chicago. "Lite" model also available.

Zigo Leader X2 Carrier Bicycle. $1,625, includes one five-point harness. Internally geared hub (Shimano Nexus). Drum brakes. "Child pod" can be removed and used as a stroller or trailer. Bike portion can be used as a bike (20-inch wheels).

Trade-Offs

Advantages: Unmatched stability; cargo capacity.

Disadvantages: Expense; weight and size; unmatched slowness.

CHAPTER 11

Long-Tail Cargo Bikes

Long Bikes, Short Years

With the motto "ride bikes, carry stuff," the Xtracycle company gave birth to the category in 1999 when they started selling conversion kits that turned regular bikes into long-tail cargo haulers. These extendo kits became pretty popular. You'd see old mountain bikes outfitted with them all over the place in Colorado.

After a while, following companies like Kona and Surly, Xtracycle started selling complete cargo bikes, sturdy steel rigs with super-long wheelbases, looking a bit like mountain bikes with stretched-out rear ends and long, stout racks on the back. Sales took off as urban families around the United States flocked to long-tail cargo bikes as their car-replacing vehicle of choice. Long-tails are a peculiarly North American phenomenon. They are especially popular in the Pacific Northwest, in Portland, Seattle, and Vancouver.

Multi-kid hauling is where these long-tails really show their worth. You can put two kids on the back deck. They can sit right on the deck—if they're big enough to hold themselves up and won't be nodding off to sleep while doing so. (Xtracycle sells a handrail that goes all the way around the cargo area that *just might* prevent a sleeping child from falling off, but maybe not.)

Haulin': Long-tail cargo bikes move kids and cargo in a variety of configurations. This Xtracycle is equipped with rails and a Yepp seat, grocery-stuffed saddle bags, and an electric motor. *Courtesy Xtracycle*

The Xtracycle EdgeRunner 24D can be equipped with all the kid-hauling accessories. *Courtesy Xtracycle*

You can attach little handlebars to the seat post so they can hold on. If they're still babies, you can put them in a seat that attaches to the deck. Then they graduate to no seat when they're big enough.

The typical cargo bike can handle two child seats in back, in addition to one up front. That's a lot of baby. Plus cargo! Stop at the grocery store on the way home, no problem. The saddle bags of long-tail bikes are designed (at least, they should be designed) not only to carry a full load of groceries but also to keep passengers' feet and hands out of the spokes. The major brands have done a good job with this safety feature. Spoke invasions have been a big source of bike-related injuries to children for as long as kids have been riding around on the backs of bicycles, but we rarely hear of long bikes having any problems with that.

There is a notable exception. In 2013 the previous version of Yuba's long-tail, the Mundo, was recalled after a few reports of kids getting their feet caught in the spokes.[1] Customers were offered a free wheel guard, aka wheelskirt, with installation. Newer models are equipped with wheelskirts as standard equipment, as all long-tails should be.

Long-tails manage to carry multiple children and still feel like bikes, cornering easily and stopping relatively well. That's the real attraction for many parents. Unloaded, the long-tail cargo bike handles better than a *bakfiets*. In fact, it handles well enough to ride trails and rough dirt roads. Don't expect it to feel like a normal bike though. The long wheelbase that makes it so stable also makes it harder to climb hills or accelerate from a stop. And then there's the weight. You'll feel the heft of all those super-stout long tubes and those burly wheels; a complete long-tail without cargo weighs about 45 or 50 pounds. Less than a bakfiets but more than a typical bike with a seat attached. So the gearing becomes much more important and necessary than it is on a regular bike. It's more like riding two bikes. The long-tail is also a lot easier to deal with than a bakfiets or trike—you can get it through a doorway. But it's still much more unwieldy than a regular bike.

Long-tails do fairly well in slippery conditions—not great, though some claim better than a traditional bakfiets, unloaded. Carrying a load, the long-tail starts to get sketchy, whereas the loaded bakfiets actually becomes more stable. Trailers are problematic on ice. This looks like a wash for the long-tail, neither advantage nor disadvantage. The three-wheeler, of course, is the only type of machine in this book that owns a clear advantage in slippery conditions.

One of the clear advantages to the long-tail is its relative affordability. Not cheap, but much cheaper than a good bakfiets. This is especially true of the Xtracycle kits, which turn old mountain bikes into passable cargo bikes. The kits are less expensive than you would expect, but remain pricier than good trailers.

"I've carried my daughter in seats, in trailers, and on the back of my Big Dummy," says Clarise Jenkins, kid-hauler extraordinaire, referring to Surly's long-tail model. "The long-tail feels the best to me, the most like a bike." This is a pretty typical reaction from people who have progressed through the different options. They become believers in long bike Xceptionalism.

With so many satisfied users talking them up and defending them, discussions about the advantages and disadvantages of long bikes can get pretty heated. But some disadvantages to these bikes have become apparent even to the most dedicated supporters. We might even come up with a few that haven't been discussed much at all. Like this one: Putting a child in a seat that attaches directly to the rack of a cargo bike could potentially give the child one heck of a rough ride, if you're not careful. In that position the kid will get jarred by bumps and rough road that you, sitting on the seat in the middle of the long frame, may not even notice. This could be a big problem for your kid. On the other hand, maybe we don't hear much about this because it's not a big deal.

The truth is that the issue is simply not well understood (see "Excessive Vibration" on page 21). Toddlers sitting on the deck itself may get excessively jostled as well, although it won't matter as much at their advanced age, and they will be better equipped to mitigate uncomfortable vibration, by adjusting body position, yelling at you to stop, etc.

Having the kids in back, rather than in front of you, is viewed by nearly all experienced family bikers as a disadvantage, because it is so much harder to hear them, talk to them, or see what they are doing back there. Not only is this a detriment to the safety of you and your kids (because, among other reasons, it forces you to frequently turn around, taking your eyes off the road and all the potential hazards ahead more often), it also leads to more strife between the kids. Point bakfiets.

Stated maximum cargo capacity on these tends to be 200 pounds, which means the bike should be able to handle two or three kids and lots of groceries easily. Long bikes can handle big weight. That's a positive. Unfortunately, things can get real dicey real quick on long-tails carrying loads of over 100 pounds. Just because the bike can handle all that weight doesn't mean you can. Depending on the rider, effective cargo capacity is likely to be much lower than the stated 200 pounds.

New Meaning to "Dropping the Kids Off at School"

What happens to a long-tail cargo bike when its pilot can't control the load? The bike tips over, and its passengers get dumped off. This occurs more frequently than you might realize. It usually happens when the rider is trying to get on the loaded bike while holding it up, or is starting on a hill. "For some reason," reported one family biker with experience across different platforms, "bikes with the load on the back are much easier for us to tip."[2] That reason is physics.

Cargo bikers have understood this seeming paradox since the early days of the bicycle: Loaded bikes are easier to control when the weight is over the front rather than the rear wheel. Putting the weight over the front wheel actually makes the steering more sensitive. This works okay, because balancing a bike is achieved by minute steering adjustments of the front wheel. Putting weight on the back makes the steering sluggish and the bike more difficult to balance. But a rider of average ability should still be able to adjust to the long-tail's funky handling—if they can get it rolling.

Some folks say that a heavy load must be balanced well on a long-tail, or it won't be safely rideable. That means if you've got something heavy on one side of the bike (say a kids' bicycle), you have to put something heavy on

MAKE YOUR OWN LONG-TAIL RAIN COVER

There's no rain cover available for your little passengers on the long-tail unless you can, as they say, cobble something up. Many have gone the DIY route, with varying results. Some of their solutions are quick and dirty, others complex and refined.

Check out these online sources for inspiration and ideas:

A simple rain cover hack for a child seat: http://youaintgotjack.blogspot.ca/p/diy-childs-bike-seat-weather-protection.html

A pram cover conversion: http://makingconcretejungle.wordpress.com/2014/02/05/diy-yuba-rain-cover-to-keep-the-kids-dry/

A labor-intensive "bike yurt": "The only thing I've made that took longer and more work were my children! But three weeks of late night sewing vigils have now paid off. The bike yurt is done." http://longwalktogreen.blogspot.com/search?q=yurt

the other side for ballast. In general, loading a long-tail requires careful consideration. That's another advantage for the box bikes, which can be loaded without much care. In reality it is not likely that you will encounter too many situations that require you to carry one heavy object in the bag of your long bike, but you may feel the bike going out of balance when your kid starts fidgeting around back there. "My kid is always trying to look around me and it throws the bike off," notes Clarise Jenkins. Movement in the wrong direction at the wrong time could be a bad scene. The low-slung bakfiets is less sensitive to cargo shifts.

We already acknowledged the long-tail's relatively okay utility in winter conditions. However, it's worth noting that the typical long-tail setup, in which kids are sitting on the rear rack, leaves them mostly unprotected should the bike slip out because of ice, or for any other reason. There is a nifty handrail among the Xtracycle accessories (called the Hooptie) that goes all the way around the cargo rack. Though much better than no rail at all, the protection it offers to passengers in a fall is not exactly complete. They're probably going to get hurt, to some degree. Trailers can do nasty things to you on ice, but at least the occupants will be relatively safe if your bike slips out.

Kids on the back of long-tails are also unprotected from the elements— the air and the stuff falling out of it. We know: "They ain't gonna melt!" But

> Americans are rear-loaders.
> —Patrick Barber, Portland (highly experienced kid-hauler and astute cultural observer)

this is certainly another point against the long-tail and in favor of the trailer or stylishly rain-canopied bakfiets or trike. It's a bit of a mystery why Xtracycle or some other company hasn't released a long-tail rain cover. (See sidebar for information about making your own.)

Long-tails have some peculiar mechanical issues too. Those chains sure are long. Under load such a long chain can sort of slap up and down when you pedal. Chain tensioners are often necessary on long-tails with hub gearing. Any time someone elongates the rear of a bike, the drivetrain's going to get elongated right along with it. No getting around that. The Europeans have always avoided elongating their drivetrains. Front-loading cargo bikes have normal bicycle drivetrains, which aids their utility.

The idea of the long-tail cargo bike must certainly have occurred to many in the past 150 years. But, for some reason(s), the idea never caught on until recently. Through decades of trial and error in the twentieth century, industrial pedalers teamed up with bike makers to develop many machines designed to carry big loads. In the majority of cases, the cargo was placed in front of the rider on a bicycle with a normal drivetrain. When the load was behind the rider, it was in a trailer or the box of a cargo trike. *Bakfietsen*, trailers, and trikes have very long histories. Long-tails? Long-tail history begins roughly fifteen years ago. There's something funky going on there.

Still, family bikers love their long bikes. And they have good reasons for that.

Buyer's Guide

Maybe the biggest reason for the long-tail's relative popularity in the United States has to do with its availability. A lot of bike shops have these things hanging around right now. You could probably test ride one and buy it today. On the other hand, most Americans would have to travel hundreds of miles, at least, to find the nearest bakfiets for sale in a retail shop. Does availability drive demand? Does lack of availability keep Dutch cargo bikes "out of sight, out of mind?" Or is some inherent American love for long bikes forcing bike shop owners to keep more in stock? It's one of those chicken-or-the-egg things.

In any case, getting your hands on a long-tail should be pretty easy. If they're not in stock at a shop that carries one of the common brand names listed below, they can be ordered without a problem. If you live around a big city, you should be able to try out a few different models before buying at your leisure. There aren't a lot of different models to choose from in this category, so it's possible that you could try out every one of the big names before making a choice.

Xtracycle's and Surly's long-tail cargo bikes are built on the "Longtail standard design platform," meaning that racks and accessories from either company will work on either company's bikes. Xtracycle has a large catalog of cool add-ons, so that's a nice arrangement for Surly Big Dummy owners.

Having observed the handling issues with loaded long bikes, Xtracycle made their EdgeRunners (like the Madsen bucket bike listed below) with a smaller rear wheel than Surly's or Yuba's. The 20-inch wheel puts the kids lower and makes the bike more stable, mitigating some of the handling shenanigans associated with long-tails. "The smaller wheel also allows its axle to be further rearward than other longtails having the same overall length. The handling improvements of a load borne lower and more completely between the axles is hard to overstate," says one retailer.[3] There is an interesting disadvantage associated with that too. It allows some kids to drag their feet on the ground! Here's one reviewer's cautionary tale: "When my daughter complained that the bike was going too fast, my son (who is now seven) responded by dragging his feet on the ground to brake the bike. It was a very effective technique, and he found my annoyance so entertaining that he did it for much of the ride. . . . So with older kids, adding footrests (to the Xtracycle EdgeRunner) is definitely not optional, and for intractable kids, this bike might not ever be the right choice."[4] Our kid isn't tall enough to do this, thankfully, or the little troublemaker would be dragging her sneakers and chortling the whole way.

The array of Xtracycle models can get confusing, especially when shops often build up bikes with unusual component mixes to put on the showroom floor. The bare-bones Xtracycle EdgeRunner comes with the wooden deck on the rack, saddlebags, and cargo kickstand. When you add the family accessories, it piles another $300 or so onto the price tag. Note that this does not include the price of a Yepp seat or seats that can be fitted niftily to the Xtracycle rack.

Budget buyers who love the long-tail idea can consider buying one of the Xtracycle kits (the new generation of which will be called the Leap) to convert an old mountain bike into a long-tail. They're cheaper, though not exactly cheap. You might also find a used Xtracycle Radish, an unusual offering that is no longer manufactured. It's an Xtracycle kit paired to an Xtracycle-branded bike with a normal wheelbase. Getting the Radish is like getting two bikes in one. The criticism of these Xtracycle kits is the same as always—that the resulting contraptions are inherently noodly when loaded.

Kona used to be a player in this long-tail market with their popular Ute model. However, the Ute seems to be discontinued, and it also seems the company is putting all their family biking eggs in one basket with a "mid-tail" bike called the MinUte. It remains to be seen how popular this new mid-tail category will be, but some of the bike companies are hoping it's the next big thing—or the next slightly less-big thing.

Mid-tails are a little cheaper and easier to handle than long-tails, which is the main attraction. Many families will appreciate the mid-tail's multi-modal potential, which is far better than the long-tail's. For instance, simply flipping the front wheel around 180-degrees makes the mid-tail short enough to fit on a bus rack. The mid-tail's cargo capacity tends to be about the same as the long-tail's, in terms of weight. That's huge. Er, small.

There are some negative consequences to shortening that wheelbase. Realistically, you're not going to fit as many grommets comfortably on a mid-tail's rack. And really heavy loads will feel even less stable than they do on a long-tail.

The mid-tail could be a good option for someone who needs to carry one kid along with lots of cargo. But if you're just carrying one kid and not messing around with groceries or other cargo, then no cargo bike, long- or mid-tail, will be worth much more than any functional bicycle sitting in your garage.

If you're intrigued by the mid-tails, check out the Kinn Cascade Flyer, handmade in Portland. Kinn offers buyers a choice between derailleurs or an 8-speed Shimano geared hub on a chromoly steel bike that sports a big ol' rack and a competitive price. On the downside, it lacks many useful kid-hauling features. Surprisingly, standard equipment doesn't include any sort of spoke guard other than the rails of the rack itself. This seems like a strange oversight for a bike that is marketed as a kid hauler. Why not sell it with some rudimentary but effective 135-degree wheel guard, as found on many basic Dutch bikes?

Yuba makes one of these mid-tails, the Boda Boda, as well as a popular long-tail model called the Mundo (world in Spanish), which costs quite a bit less than the Big Dummy or Xtracycle. Unfortunately the big Mundo has V-brakes, disappointing cargo bikers of the rainy Northwest. It is, at least, disc brake–ready. The Mundo only comes in one size, but owners tend not to have many problems with that. (At least, we haven't heard any complaints.) The mid-tail Boda Boda needs some add-ons before you can carry kids with it. The big Mundo comes standard with many of the family-oriented accessories you need, but maybe not all of them. Most notably, the Mundo now comes with wheelskirts, which is very good.

Trek used to be in the long-tail cargo bike market, but for some reason decided to get out. Trek's Transport was an aluminum-framed long-tail, on the expensive side, and by all accounts a pretty nice bike, though more cargo-oriented than kid-friendly. People liked it. But not enough people, apparently, as Trek has disappeared it from their lineup. (As of October 2015 the Transport does not appear on Trek's website, www.trekbikes .com/us/en/bikes/city/.) If you're looking for a used long-tail, remember the Transport.

A special note on the Madsen cargo bike listed below: The Madsen could be called a long-tail, but it's very different from the Big Dummy, Xtracycle EdgeRunner, Yuba Mundo, or Trek Transport. Rather than a rack over the rear wheel, the Madsen has a cargo bucket sitting between the rider and its 20-inch rear wheel. This puts the cargo weight much lower, which is nice. You can just put the kid(s) in there with some additional cargo and not worry too much about balancing the load, similar to a front-loading bakfiets. On the other hand, the rear wheel encroaches a bit into the cargo space, and this has been an annoying issue for some owners.

Rear-loading bucket bikes like the Madsen and the rare 8Freight are more committed cargo-haulers, with the usual lack of snazzy handling associated with that. The EdgeRunner and other Xtracycle-inspired long-tails handle well when unloaded. The Madsen is a slow troller even when unloaded.

After some years Madsen finally responded to complaints from owners and released a rain canopy for their cargo bucket, but it's expensive. The bike

ELECTRIC ASSIST

Just about any of the cargo bikes listed in this book, from long-tails to "Long Johns" and trikes, can be retrofitted with an electric motor. Many can be purchased with an electric motor already installed. It makes sense when you realize how heavy these bikes are to begin with, and how difficult it can be to pedal a loaded cargo bike uphill.

Electric assist isn't just for lazy dawdlers, as many may assume. Electric assist is serious business for serious transportation cycling. Many families consider their electric motors to be absolutely essential parts of their daily transportation, critical components that allow them to do what they do. Family bikers who live in hilly cities like San Francisco or Seattle increasingly cherish electric assist systems. If you have a lot of hills in your family biking universe, have multiple children to haul around, or want a little boost as you embark on a car-free life, e-assist might be for you.

Today's electric motor isn't anything like the Briggs & Stratton go-cart engine that eccentric old guy down the block put on his "10-speed" back in the day so he could boogie loudly to the 7-11 for smokes. These motors are silent, stinkless, and very sophisticated. And they're being improved constantly as American cargo bikers push them to their limits on the steep hills of the West Coast.

Unfortunately the latest, greatest electric assist systems are extremely expensive. From $1,500 to $2,500 dollars is typical for the good stuff. Add that to the already pricey cargo bike on which it's installed and you're well into car territory. Again, you could certainly get a nice used Camry and a top-of-the-line car seat—and even have plenty left over for gasoline—for the price of a good cargo bike with e-assist. That doesn't mean you shouldn't get the bike, but it's something to think about, especially if saving money is your primary motivation for using a bike instead of a car. Of course bicycling comes with all sorts of advantages and positive consequences that drivers can only dream about, so price is just one factor to consider.

BionX (sounds like "bionics") has been assuming control of the North American market. BionX e-assist systems, made in Canada, deliver power when the rider is pedaling—"pedal-assist." They can also be kitted up with a throttle, allowing riders to cruise along under motor power while coasting. BionX systems have their motor at the rear hub, so a special rear wheel is part of the package. Other popular systems are "mid-drive," with the motor attached to the frame near the bottom bracket.

There is one huge advantage to the hub motor: It lets you turn just about any bike into an e-bike. It also allows you to replace the wheel with your old regular wheel at any time and instantly get that old bike back. That's a huge contrast to mid-drive systems, which require special frames.

BionX systems have four power settings. On the lowest setting the motor adds another 25 percent or so to whatever level of power the rider is supplying, automatically measured by a sensor in the hub. At the highest setting it adds up to 300 percent, depending on specific models. In other words, they are capable of quadrupling the rider's power output. BionX systems also have a generator mode that adds resistance to pedaling while charging the battery. The lithium-ion batteries are available in two basic

BionX pedal-assist systems consist of a special rear wheel, a large battery that can be mounted on the frame, and a throttle switch and display/control unit that mount on the handlebar. BionX systems are known for adding power to a rider's pedal strokes, but also allow the user to motor along under power without pedaling.
Courtesy BionX

types: rear rack-mount or downtube-mount. The downtube-mounted battery, looking like a huge water bottle on the frame, is the most popular setup for cargo bikers. Range at full charge is about 40 miles for the least powerful model and well over 60 for the most powerful BionX available (in North America). With battery, motor, and console, BionX systems add about 15 to 20 pounds to a bike's weight, depending on the system in question.

The ECO PL 250M is the least powerful BionX system, with a 250-watt motor and a price around $1,500. Other systems have more range, more assist power, more weight, and bigger price tags.

To illustrate just how far we've gone down the digital highway, software determines the finer points of the BionX system's operation. Several parameters can be tweaked to customize the system. However, to adjust the software or download updates, the user must go to a BionX dealer.

The highly respected German company Bosch is also heavily into the e-assist game. Bosch uses a mid-drive motor. Unlike the BionX, the Bosch motor can't be retrofitted onto a regular bike, but requires a dedicated frame. The mid-drive motor has a small sprocket that drives the bike's chain, whereas motors like the BionX turn the hub. While the hub motor allows for regenerative braking, the Bosch does not. Other than that it gives the same basic results as the hub motor, with sensors and pedal-assist power up to 350 watts. You'll find the Bosch on many popular European e-bikes. It's available in the United States, and many big manufacturers, like Xtracycle, are making complete bikes built around the Bosch mid-drive motor. Other names, like Currie Technologies, can be found on e-motors in the United States, but as we write this the contest for this burgeoning North American market looks like it's shaping up to be BionX versus Bosch. It'll be interesting to see how it shakes out.

Note that North American regulations require an e-assist system to stop assisting once the rider reaches 20 miles per hour. That's probably for the best. You don't want or need to be going faster than 20 miles per hour on flat land while carrying kids or cargo. Twenty doesn't sound too sexy, but it's faster than most of us realize. Some e-bike makers are selling rigs that will pedal-assist at higher speeds, relying on a loophole in the regulations that allows—for some inexplicable reason—faster speeds for off-street use, on trails and bike paths. But 20 is more than plenty for family biking.

We hear many criticisms of e-bikes, but perhaps the most valid concerns are about safety. Going faster is not always better. The faster you ride, the less likely it is that motorists will see you. The faster you ride, the less time you will have to avoid inevitable intrusions. The faster you ride, the more violent a collision will be, with more aggravated injuries. If saving time is the primary motivation for your move to e-assist, maybe it would be easier to just leave 10 minutes earlier. It would definitely be safer. Fortunately most of the family bikers who spend the cash on electronic assist systems aren't really interested in going fast.

It's easy to criticize e-assist and the riders who use it—if you haven't pedaled a mile in somebody else's shoes. Pedal-assist systems are practical, helpful, even crucial equipment for some family bikers. Imagine yourself with three kids in your cargo box. With the kids, the bike, and your own body, that could be 300-plus pounds to move. Add gravity to the equation, and e-assist may be the only thing that allows you to reach the top of the hill. Or the middle of it. Imagine the pregnant woman with two kids on the back of a long bike—and they're all stopping at the grocery store on the way home. She might need that motor just to keep from dumping the bike.

Like it or not, e-assist is leaking into middle America.

itself is around two grand, including bucket and shipping, so a lot of families with bakfiets dreams and long-tail budgets have gone with the Madsen. Their reviews of the bike, however, have been mixed.

The big manufacturers all offer electrified versions of their bikes, or the rigs can be modified later with mounts that have been built into the frames. E-assist compatibility is something the long-tail companies really focus on, with their core customer base concentrated in super-hilly West Coast cities. E-assist is massively expensive. The favored kits of 2015 run about $2,000 (long whistle). You can get an old, used Lexus for the same price of an e-assist long-tail. We're not suggesting you should get the car instead, but it might be useful to notice these things (see "Electric Assist" on page 132). Watch for new dedicated cargo e-bikes from Yuba and Xtracycle, using Currie Technologies and Bosch motors, respectively.

With the possible exception of the Surly Big Dummy, with its Shimano Deore derailleurs and hubs, the mass-market long-tails are spec'd with some relatively low-end components. The component lists are what you usually find on sub-$1,000 bikes. So you're paying for cargo capacity and current trendiness. The makers and retailers are usually right when they figure that the people who are shopping for these family bikes don't know much about components and won't really care which they get as long as they work reasonably well.

If you're thinking about getting one of these long-tail haulers, whether the Xtracycle, Madsen, or any others, do what you can to try it out first, with cargo if possible. They are quirky enough machines that some (among the incredible variety of riders who make up the family biking army) are sure to love them, while others will really dislike them. You just don't want to find out that you're one of those long-tail haters about two weeks after dropping $3,000 on one sight unseen.

Check with the manufacturers for specifics like full component lists and frame geometry. Remember: Prices are approximations, taken from retailers at the time this book was written. Bicycle prices vary widely from shop to shop, and prices listed by any retailer are subject to change.

Product List

Azor Long Tail. $1,599, includes built-in rack, cargo kickstand, chain case, fenders, and generator lights. Steel mid-tail frame. Internally geared hub (Shimano Nexus 8-speed). Roller brakes (unspecified). Looks like an elongated Dutch bike. Well, that's exactly what it is; it's handmade in Holland. Few distributors in the United States.

Kinn Cascade Flyer (mid-tail). $2,350, includes rack, kickstand, fenders, foot pegs, and Brooks saddle. Two sizes. Steel mid-tail frame. Choice of derailleur gearing (Shimano Alivio front, Deore rear, 27-speed) or internally geared hub (Shimano Alfine 8-speed). Mechanical disc brakes front and rear (Avid BB5). Handmade in Portland, Oregon.

Kona MinUte (mid-tail). $1,399, includes built-in rack with wooden deck, saddle bags, steering stabilizer, fenders, and cargo kickstand. Two frame sizes. Aluminum mid-tail frame. Mechanical disc brakes front and rear (Tektro). Derailleur gearing (Shimano Acera rear, Altus front). Only one color scheme: charcoal gray and white. Good package of accessories but some cheapie parts.

Madsen. $1,875, not including shipping. Includes rear plastic bucket, removable seats and four seat belts, fenders, and cargo kickstand. One size. Steel frame. Derailleur gearing (SRAM X-5). Mechanical disc brake front (Tektro), V-brake rear (Tektro). A "bucket bike," quite different from the other long-tails here. This is an Internet-only purchase. For more information: info@madsencycles.com.

Surly Big Dummy. $1,999, includes rack rails and deck and saddle bags. Four frame sizes. Steel frame. Mechanical disc brakes front and rear (Avid BB7). Derailleur gearing (Shimano Deore 3 x 9). Only one color—"asphalt gray." Compatible with Xtracycle accessories. Made in Taiwan.

Xtracycle EdgeRunner 24D. $1,999, includes saddle bags and cargo kickstand. Handrails, footrests, padded seat, fenders, and lights are extra. Two frame sizes. Steel frame (half chromoly). Derailleur gearing (Shimano Altus/M191 24-speed). Mechanical disc brakes (Tektro Aquila). 20-inch rear wheel.

Xtracycle EdgeRunner 27D. $2,399, includes saddle bags and cargo kickstand. Handrails, footrests, padded seat, fenders, and lights are extra. Two frame sizes. Steel frame (chromoly throughout). Derailleur gearing (Shimano Alivio/Acera 27-speed). Mechanical disc brakes (Avid BB7). 20-inch rear wheel.

Xtracycle EdgeRunner 30D. $2,699, includes saddle bags and cargo kickstand. Handrails, footrests, padded seat, fenders, and lights are extra. Two frame sizes. Steel frame (chromoly throughout). Derailleur gearing (Shimano Deore 30-speed). Hydraulic disc brakes (Deore). 20-inch rear wheel.

Yuba Boda Boda. $999, includes built-in cargo rack. All other kid-carrying accessories are extra. Two frame sizes. Aluminum frame. Derailleur gearing (SRAM X-3 8-speed). V-brakes front and rear (Promax). Shorter than a long-tail and a bit lighter, called a "mid-tail." Styled to look and ride like a Dutch city bike.

The Yuba Boda Boda is one of several "mid-tail" cargo bikes now available. Mid-tails can haul one kid and groceries nicely, but can't do quite as much as the long-tails.
Courtesy Yuba

Yuba Mundo v4.3. $1,299, includes rack and bamboo deck, wheelskirts, footrests, fenders, and cargo kickstand. Does not include handrails, handlebars or padded seats for passengers, or cargo bags. One frame size. Steel frame. Derailleur gearing (SRAM). V-brakes front and rear (Promax). Disc-ready.

Yuba Mundo Lux. $1,499, includes rack and bamboo deck, wheelskirts, footrests, fenders, cargo kickstand, generator hub (SRAM), and lights. Does not include handrails, handlebars or padded seats for passengers, or cargo bags. One frame size. Steel frame. Derailleur gearing (SRAM). Disc brakes front and rear (Tektro).

A Yuba Mundo with front basket, passenger handlebar, and rear seat. Make sure there's something covering the spokes of the rear wheel. *Courtesy Yuba*

Trade-Offs

Advantages: More affordable than a bakfiets; rides like a bike; serious cargo capacity.

Disadvantages: Less affordable than a trailer; physics of rear-loading.

CHAPTER 12

Trailer Bikes

Pedal Trailers

We just kind of made up that term. There really is no consensus on what to call these things. They are often referred to as "trail-a-bikes" in the United States, but that's really a brand name that should be capitalized.

A trailer bike is essentially the back end of a child's bicycle, which can be attached to a regular adult bicycle, thus creating a tandem with three in-line wheels. Like many others, this idea can be traced back at least to the 1890s. The concept was refined in the 1930s by Bill Rann in England, where trailer bikes are still known to many old-schoolers as "Rann trailers."

The function of the device depends in large part on the design and placement of the pivoting joint between the bike and the trailer. Quite simply, some designs work better than others. But those better designs are also more expensive to build. When trailer bikes experienced a renaissance in the 1980s, many cheap models with lesser designs came on the market. As Tony Hadland and Hans-Erhard Lessing note in *Bicycle Design*: "Most designs used the simple and cheap expedient of coupling the trailer to the bicycle's seat post. This could work reasonably well if the pivot was vertical and was

Weehoo trailers are a cool combination of trailer bike and trailer. Since the passenger sits in a bucket seat and harness while pedaling, Weehoo trailers can be used with younger kids than would be possible with a regular trailer bike.
Courtesy Weehoo

TRAILER BIKE RECALLS

Recalls have affected several of the top brands, even a few we recommend here.

- Over 4,000 Hitchhiker III Trailer Bikes by InSTEP, sold at Toys R Us, Sports Authority, and other retail stores in 2001, were recalled after the company received ten reports of broken universal joints (the hitch system), resulting in minor injuries. Affected customers were offered a repair kit and instructions. ("CPSC, InSTEP LLC Announce Recall of Trailer Bikes," CPSC, April 25, 2002, Release #02-148, www.cpsc.gov/en/Recalls/2002/CPSC-InSTEP-LLC-Announce-Recall-of-Trailer-Bikes/.)

- About 300 Taiwan-built 2005 Nashbar Lil' Shadow Tandem Trailers, which were improperly assembled, were recalled. No injuries were reported. Nashbar offered affected customers a full refund and a $20 gift certificate. ("CPSC, Nashbar Direct Announce Recall of Bicycle Trailers," CPSC, June 20, 2005, Alert #05-581.)

- After a single report of a Novara Afterburner trailer bike uncoupling from the adult bicycle to which it had been attached, over 5,000 units were recalled in 2007. REI offered customers a choice of a replacement part, full refund, or store credit. ("REI Recalls Children's Trailer Bicycles; Can Detach from Adult Bicycle and Injure Children," CPSC, September 18, 2007, Alert #07-578, www.cpsc.gov/en/Recalls/2007/REI-Recalls-Childrens-Trailer-Bicycles-Can-Detach-from-Adult-Bicycle-and-Injure-Children/.)

- This 2008 recall concerned cheaper models of "trailer bicycles" made in China for Pacific Cycle Inc. of Madison, Wisconsin,

bracketed out from the seat post clamp toward the rear axle. If, however, the pivoting was around the seat post, the geometry was very bad, the trailer being made to lean out of the turn while the bike leaned in. And some seats weren't strong enough to cope with the loads."[1]

The trailer bike is fundamentally problematic from a handling standpoint, and the problems can be badly exacerbated by poor design, which is something to think about if you're considering getting one of these things.

and sold as the InStep "Pathfinder," Schwinn "Run About," and Mongoose "Alley Cat." One incident was reported in which the coupler failed, dumping a kid onto the pavement. The welds on the coupler were found to be failure-prone, and Pacific offered customers free repair kits to fix the issue. ("Pacific Cycle Recalls Children's Trailer Bicycles; Can Detach from Adult Bicycle and Injure Children," CPSC, January 8, 2008, Release #08-156, www .cpsc.gov/en/Recalls/2008/Pacific-Cycle-Recalls-Childrens -Trailer-Bicycles-Can-Detach-from-Adult-Bicycle-and-Injure -Children/.)

- Weehoo of Golden, Colorado, recalled about 2,700 of their iGo bicycle pedal trailers after a single report of the trailer's receiver cracking. No injury was involved. The parts were manufactured in Taiwan during a few months in 2011. Customers were instructed to contact Weehoo for a free reinforcement sleeve. ("Weehoo Recalls Bike Trailers Due to Fall and Crash Hazards," CPSC, September 13, 2011, Release #11-323, www.cpsc.gov/en/Recalls/2011/ Weehoo-Recalls-Bike-Trailers-Due-to-Fall-and-Crash-Hazards/.)

- In late 2013 Burley Design recalled its Tailwind racks for Trailercycles after receiving numerous reports of the racks breaking. Two injuries were reported, including a leg fracture. The company offered to replace customers' Tailwind racks with a beefier model free of charge. ("Burley Design Recalls Tailwind Racks for Trailercycles Due to Fall Hazard," CPSC, November 26, 2013, Recall #14-033, www.cpsc.gov/en/Recalls/2014/ Burley-Design-Recalls-Tailwind-Racks-for-Trailercycles/.)

Indeed, many users are disappointed by the feel of the contraption when they use it for the first time. "It flops around back there," they report, which is an exaggeration but gives you a good idea of the basic issue.

So why do trailer bikes even exist? Why do they not only exist but remain a force in the industry? Because they fill a need for many parents that's difficult to satisfy in other ways. When a child reaches a certain age—certainly old enough to hold on for long periods of time and not fall asleep—it makes sense to get them more actively involved. At the same time, they're not ready to pilot their own bikes. During such a phase, a family tandem is an extremely practical option. (See the "Family Tandems" chapter). Unfortunately, family tandems—tandems in general—are expensive. That's where the trailer bike comes in, providing many of the benefits of the family tandem without the price.

Buyer's Guide

Again we recommend avoiding the really cheap offerings online and at discount megastores. Trailer bikes are problematic enough when they're done well. You don't want to mess with bargain imitations. Luckily, if you're looking for a good deal, it's pretty easy to find quality trailer bikes on craigslist, and at bike swaps or other used marketplaces.

A lot of parents buy these when their kids turn 4 or so, then find that the poor child isn't big enough to even reach the pedals. Don't get too ambitious about putting younger kids on trailer bikes before their time—it'll just end in heartache. For kids who are ready, but just very small, crank shorteners can allow the child to reach the bottom of the pedal stroke.

Take note of the different types of hitches. The Burley models come with a rear rack for the adult's bicycle, and the hitch is on the rack, directly over the rear axle. This is the Rann design, long ago determined to be best for handling and control. And they own the patent on that. Having to use a rack comes with a little extra installation hassle, however. The seat post hitches used by almost every other manufacturer are easier, but floppier and clumsier.

The Burleys are relatively lightweight, and each can be converted to a full bicycle with the purchase of a $159 kit. The Trail-a-Bikes are heavier but cheaper and also foldable, a nice feature allowing for easy transport of the machine to remote locations.

For something really different in this category, check out the Weehoo iGo trailers. These don't look or act like the others. The Weehoo is sort of the recumbent version of the trailer bike, on which the kid sits in a bucket seat at axle level, pedaling a set of cranks in front of the seat. This design allows the kid to doze off or just sit back and relax. Weehoo trailers are a bit more expensive than traditional trailer bikes.

A unique product we really like is the FollowMe Tandem Coupling, a device that allows just about any kid's bike to be towed by the parent's bike—so the kid can stay on her own bike, with no worries about adjusting or growing into the trailer bike. This lets kids ride tandem sooner than they would be able to otherwise. The FollowMe is expensive, however, so it's not really a money-saver.

Product List

Burley Kazoo. $299. Aluminum frame. Single speed. Weight: 16.5 pounds. Includes rack. Trailer attaches to hitch on the rack, directly over the rear axle. Can be converted to complete bicycle.

The single-speed Burley Kazoo. Burley owns the patent on the rack-mounted linkage, which gives the 3-wheeled machine more stability. *Courtesy Burley*

Burley Piccolo. $359. Aluminum frame. 7-speed drivetrain. Weight: 18 pounds. Includes rack. Trailer attaches to hitch on the rack, directly over the rear axle. Can be converted to complete bicycle.

The Burley Piccolo has a derailleur and gears. *Courtesy Burley*

FollowMe Tandem Coupling. $399. Weight: 9 pounds. Allows the adult bike to tow the child's bike like a trailer. Works for kids' bikes with 12- to 20-inch wheels.

Novara Afterburner 2.0. $249. Steel frame. Single-speed. Weight: 24 pounds. Seat post hitch.

Trail-a-Bike Folder One. $225. Steel frame. Single-speed. Weight: 23.5 pounds. Seat post hitch. Folding frame.

Trail-a-Bike Folder Compact. $225. Steel frame. Single-speed. Weight: 23 pounds. Seat post hitch. Folding frame. A slightly smaller version of the original, with shorter reach, smaller cranks and chainring, and narrower handlebars.

Trail-a-Bike Folder Tandem. $600. Steel frame. 7-speed drivetrain. Weight: 34 pounds. Seat post hitch. Folding frame. Tandem-style seating for two, with two sets of cranks. Weight capacity: 125 pounds.

Weehoo iGo Turbo. $399. Steel frame. Single speed. Weight: 27 pounds. Includes recumbent-style seat and cranks, saddle bags.

Securely strapped into the Weehoo pedal
Courtesy Weehoo

Weehoo iGo Two. $519. Steel frame. Single speed. Weight: 40 pounds. Includes two recumbent-style seats in-line and one set of cranks, saddle bags. Weight capacity: 100 pounds.

Weehoo iGo Venture. $519. Steel frame. Single speed. Weight: 27 pounds. Includes recumbent-style seat and cranks, saddle bags, and cargo basket. Weight capacity: 80 pounds.

The Weehoo is an intriguing option for off-roading with a kid. *Courtesy Weehoo*

WeeRide Co-Pilot. $120. Steel frame. Single speed. Weight: 24 pounds, frame alone.

Trade-Offs

Advantages: Relatively cheap family tandem substitute; kids enjoy it.

Disadvantages: Feels awkward; may bind in turns or feel floppy or loose.

CHAPTER 13

Family Tandems

A Bicycle Built For Two. Or Three. Or Four.

This is one of the smallest, and coolest, categories of family vehicles. The family tandem is an elongated bike with two to four seats, handlebars, and cranksets. Some family tandems look like traditional tandems, with the kid "stoker" sitting behind the parent "captain." Others are built very much like two-wheeled *bakfietsen*, with 20-inch wheels in the front and 26-inch wheels in the back—about 7 or 8 feet behind the front. The distant front wheel is steered by the adult driver via a rod linked to the steer tube. The child passengers have no control over steering, shifting, or braking, but they can pedal. The long-nose-style family tandem shines as a two-kid carrier. (Tandems with two extra seats are also known as "triple tandems.")

Note! Kiddie Crank Alert! Some regular, adult tandems can be converted into family tandems simply by installing "kiddie cranks." If you already own an adult tandem, or want to get one, you'll definitely want to consider its convertibility to a family tandem.

Family tandems are useful for families with kids who are old enough to hold on and pedal, but not quite ready to ride by themselves. Like the trailer bike rigs, family tandems also work well for parents whose kids have

Family tandems like this Onderwater XL are extremely versatile machines. *Courtesy Ronald Onderwater* learned to ride but aren't ready to make their own decisions in traffic. It's been claimed by many parents that their kids seemed to learn a lot about safe riding just by observing while on the tandem. (See the "Teaching Kids to Ride Safely" chapter.) Some kids who are perfectly competent riders just love cruising on a tandem with their mom or dad, and will want to until middle school and beyond. (After that you might start worrying about them!)

If you're wondering if your kid is old enough to ride on one, she probably isn't. You'll know when kids are ready. Four years old or so is a general rule of thumb.

You're not really hauling kids on a family tandem. Now they can haul you a little bit. It's more of a shared experience. All part of the progression!

Families considering a tandem rig may be weighing pros and cons and comparing it with the far cheaper trailer bike setup. Unlike the trailer bike rigs, the long-nose-style family tandems put the kids in front of the parent, where the parent can easily observe and communicate with them. This is a big advantage. And tandem bicycles, since they are bicycles, ride like bikes—very long bikes—which most experienced bike handlers prefer to the clunky feel of pulling a trailer. If you're wrangling multiple grommets, keeping them all on the same machine is a more tidy arrangement than putting one child on your bike while the other trails behind, which turns the bike into a floppy semitruck. Many trailer bike setups have a sloppy feel. Family tandems are much more expensive than trailer bikes, however, and a lot harder to find in the United States.

Is it worth it? The prices of quality family tandems are not really suited to tight budgets (with the possible exception of the Bike Friday). For a bike that could simply be bridging a short gap in your kids' development, between the passenger years and pedaling years, that's an awful lot of clams. Many families use these exclusively for recreational outings, which makes the cost-per-trip very high unless they're getting out there on a constant basis. On the other hand, some families use their tandem the same way they would use a family car—which means they don't necessarily need a family car any more. Resale value should be fairly good, but probably not as strong as with a *bakfiets* or a good long-tail. Is somebody going to come along in a year or two and pick up your family tandem for more than a fraction of its original cost? Not sure about that. But they might. And your family might just enjoy this bike so much that you keep on using it for many years.

Note that some family tandems of the bakfiets variety will in fact magically transform into a Euro-style box bike, sort of almost. Theoretically you could use it as a box bike before the kid is old enough to sit on a saddle and pedal, then convert it to the tandem when she's ready, and, finally, turn it back into a box bike and sell it for a pretty penny to some hipsters like yourself after your kid is too cool to be seen on it anymore. Practically speaking, though, the boxes are stunted versions of the real thing and may not work for hauling kids.

Buyer's Guide

Being different than bakfietsen and other bikes, family tandems have a different list of necessary components for safely hauling kids. You won't be needing any seat belts or wheel covers, for instance. No $500 "family package." In general you can be more casual about outfitting the family tandem, because the kids are taking better care of themselves by the time they are old enough to ride it.

The captain of this category is the Onderwater brand. The Onderwater Family Tandem XL is classic Dutch machinery, but the average American is likely to freak out a little bit just at the sight of it. There are two saddles for kids in front, where the wooden box would normally go; you can put another one directly in front of the parent's spot, behind the handlebars. A fourth kid (!) can be carried in a seat on the integrated rear rack (seat not included). The kids sitting in the front saddles have independent cranksets and pedals; they can pedal along, supplying some power, or not. A kid seated in the optional saddle directly in front of the parent won't have any pedals to play around with, just a footrest, which seems like a potential problem-causer when she notices her older siblings up front cranking away.

The Onderwaters are really cool machines because they can be turned into bakfietsen! Just remove the kids' equipment and put a cargo box up there instead. Box not included, of course. When you crunch the numbers, however (or those numbers crunch you), it's still an expensive option.

The Kidz Tandem from Brown Cycles is styled after long-nose Euro rigs. Their standard option has one extra seat, but you can also get a longer-nosed version with seats for two little stokers. Brown Cycles also offers a road version with skinny tires, drop bars, and STI shifters, and a mountain version with suspension forks and knobbies. We think the frame is the same for all versions, so don't get too excited.

The Kidz Tandem has a really interesting and useful feature: The kid's saddle can be quickly swapped out for a special car seat–like seat, allowing

A second child can be seated on this Onderwater family tandem with an optional seat that attaches in front of the parent's seat. A third can sit on the rack or a seat on the rack. *Courtesy Ronald Onderwater*

smaller kids to ride up front before they have the ability to hold on or reach the pedals. This isn't an inherently protective situation like strapping the seat into a bakfiets or trailer, so the child riding in this seat really needs to be wearing a helmet. For that reason this seat wouldn't be suitable for infants younger than 1 year old. (See the "Kids' Helmets" chapter.) Any seat meant for kids wearing helmets should have a recessed area for the helmet so it doesn't force the child's head down.

Co-Motion, like several other companies, makes conventional captain/stoker tandems that accommodate smaller riders in back. These bikes work best for older kids and parents who want to ride far and fast. Their bikes are well made.

The Bike Friday Family Tandem is an intriguing option. A more traditional captain/stoker tandem, it can be set up for one or two kids who are over 3 feet tall. (Bike Friday says it's for kids at least 4 years old.) Like other bikes made by this long-established American brand, it has 20-inch wheels and an easy-peasy low frame, and it handles with surprising zing. Bike Friday sells semi-custom bikes, so you won't really know how much it costs until all the individual choices have been made—and there are a lot of them. Note that the bike doesn't come standard with pedals and saddles—the company says it doesn't want to make that choice for you, and there's some merit to that. That's also a part of the relatively low price.

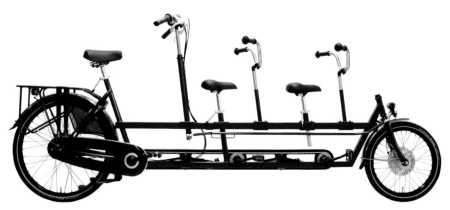

Onderwater XL, for three pedalers, handmade in the Netherlands *Courtesy Ronald Onderwater*

Bike Friday seems a little bit cagey about the exact components included as standard on its base model (that info's on the order form), which is not a good sign. It makes comparison shopping difficult. But that's typical for companies that sell bikes like this. The "specifications" tend not to be very specific. The industry's approach to selling family tandems is shaped by the fact that most people who are buying them don't care too much about the quality of the frame or components, and assume it's all pretty much the same.

People who know something about bikes and parts, and who already have a good idea of what they want, will be more comfortable shopping for a family tandem. Or more aggravated, as the case may be.

Best way to go here? The Onderwater Family Tandem—used. Pass the Dutchie. And let us know if you find one, because we'd like to buy it when you're done.

Product List

Bike Friday Family Tandem. $1,298 base price, includes one extra seat, handlebars, and crankset. Does not include kickstand, fenders, pedals, or saddles. Derailleur gearing (Shimano Altus). V-brakes front and rear (Shimano M422). Check the Bike Friday website (www.bikefriday.com/bicycles/configure/1399) to order a bike and choose alternate components. Made in Oregon.

Brown Cycles Kidz Tandem. $2,250, includes one extra saddle and crankset assembly, rear rack, fenders, and double kickstand.[1] Steel frame. Derailleur gears (unknown). V-brakes front and rear (unknown).

Co-Motion Periscope Scout. $3,495.[2] Three sizes. Steel frame. Derailleur gearing (Shimano 105 triple). Disc brakes front and rear (Avid BB7). Handmade in Oregon. A traditional captain/stoker tandem with kid in back. More performance-oriented, not cargo-oriented.

Hase Pino Allaround. $5,659, includes generator hub, lights, kickstand, SKS fenders, rear rack, and suspension fork (Spinner Grind 1, reinforced). Child's crank is extra. Aluminum frame. Derailleur gears (Shimano Deore 27-speed). Hydraulic disc brakes front and rear (Avid Code R). Made in Germany. A half-recumbent tandem. Can be set up for a child "passenger" with the purchase of optional child's crank.

Onderwater Family Tandem. $2,999, includes generator hub/light, taillight, fenders, and rear rack.[3] Seating for two kids, one up front with pedals and cranks, and another directly in front of the driver (footrest only). Option for a third child behind the driver on the rack. Internally geared hub (Shimano Nexus 8-speed). Front and rear roller brakes (unknown). Comes with an Axa Defender integrated rear wheel lock with a microchip inside. Can be fitted with a cargo box. This is a smaller version of the Onderwater XL, with a cheaper rear hub and brakes.

Onderwater Family Tandem XL. €1,899, not including shipping. Includes generator hub/light, taillight, fenders, and rear rack.[4] Seating for two kids up front, with an option for a third seat directly in front of the driver (footrest only), and a fourth behind the driver on the rack. Internally geared hub (Nuvinci continuously variable transmission). Front and rear roller brakes (Shimano IM81). Comes with an Axa Defender integrated rear wheel lock with a microchip inside. Can be fitted with a cargo box.

Trade-Offs

Advantages: Fun for all; educational for kids learning about traffic.

Disadvantages: Expense; length and lack of portability.

CHAPTER 14

Balance Bikes

How to Teach Your Kid to Ride a Bike

Teaching kids to ride bikes has never been easier, that's for sure. Basically you just obtain a "balance bike," a toddler-size bike without any pedals or drivetrain, which is propelled by the child's feet, and the machine does all the work. Almost any child using a balance bike will learn—pretty quickly too—how to balance and turn on two wheels. From there it's a short hop to pedaling a real bike like a champ. It's a proven method. Balance bike kids usually go straight to pedal bikes without bothering with training wheels. In fact, balance bikes are killing training wheels. We predict that training wheels will be all but extinct by 2030. (Nice round number.)

Older kids or even adults can learn to ride bikes using the same basic method: Just remove the pedals from and lower the seats on a regular bike to create a makeshift balance bike. Once they learn balance, put the pedals back on and off they go. Simple, effective, and fun.

Balance bikes have been growing in popularity quickly as more and more parents become clued in to their magical properties. Because of the balance bike phenomenon, the American childhood has been transformed. When we were kids, adults were intimately involved in the process of teaching children to ride a bike. At the crux of this process, that critical, ecstatic

We wish we had these when we were kids. *tatyana_tomsickova/iStock/Thinkstock*

CHRISTIE REMEMBERS LEARNING TO RIDE

Using her bushels of patience and her triathlete-like stamina, my grandmother taught me how to ride a bike. Unbeknownst to either of us at the time, she probably changed my life.

I was about 6 years old, and one of my prized possessions was my Strawberry Shortcake bike. It had a strawberry-patterned banana seat, pink handlebar grips, and training wheels. It oozed the essence of the cloying, ginger-haired doll that consumed me back in those halcyon days of first grade—that time before life got complicated with high expectations and drama in second grade.

I loved that bike. I spent hours tooling back and forth on the sidewalk in front of my grandmother's house. I rode up and down the alley behind her house too. The alley became one of my favorite places to ride because it wasn't so busy and it offered a unique perspective of our inner-city Baltimore neighborhood. You could smell other peoples' cooking and look at their gardens. It was quiet. It was a place where a girl could think.

At some point my grandmother decided the training wheels needed to go. I was nervous—those wheels were my safety net. But on the other hand, I always felt oddly unsteady with them. They didn't touch the ground at the same time, so I wobbled while I rode. And with an extra wheel always dragging, I felt sluggish. Those hard plastic training wheels made a distinct noise as they scraped on the ground. It was the sound of *slow*. So my grandfather removed the wheels, and the rest was up to Grandma.

I don't remember how many days she jogged back and forth in the alley, gripping the back of the seat, coaching me on. Poor Grandma. It didn't occur to me at the time that she would rather have been chatting away in the living room with a glass of Gallo

moment when we broke through to the other side and learned how to keep the bicycle upright, many of us remember a parent (or, in Christie's case, a grandparent) running along right there next to us. It became a cherished memory for parent and child alike.

If there's anything negative to say about balance bikes, it concerns their propensity to steal precious memories.

wine in one hand and a stuffed mushroom cap in the other, the fancy lady she was.

I do remember the exact moment she let go, I mean, really let go. I was on my own, sailing down the alley. No training wheels to slow me, no hand on the seat to steady me. I felt the Zen of my balance and my pedaling and the wind. My life changed in that moment. I felt . . . perfection.

I've been riding almost constantly during the thirty-some years since that day. Sometimes I can recapture that moment when it all comes together—the balance, the pedaling, and the wind. Almost like a junkie now, I'm chasing the perfect high: riding every day, using my bike to manage stress, to stay fit, to commute, to have fun, and best of all, to get that Zen thing going.

Sadly, Grandma passed away a few years ago. Hours before she died, I did get to thank her for teaching me to ride a bike. I told her how it changed my life, and how grateful I was for that, and for her.

With the advent of balance bikes, these moments of connection between kids and family members might be almost gone. That's sad, because in my quest to get my daughter to like me best and to remember me better than anyone else, what's left? Teaching her to Tweet?

She cruises around on her balance bike like a mini Jeannie Longo. She doesn't need me! But for now I run next to her and at least pretend that she does. And when she gets older we can ride together. And when she gets even older and I'm really old, maybe we can get a mother-daughter tandem. She can take the front because of my failing eyesight. She can help me chase that moment of Zen perfection, right up to the end.

Beside those lovely memories, however, the old way of learning to ride left much to be desired. Little kids were stuck. Stuck with training wheels. The problem with training wheels is they don't do much training. A kid pedaling along, leaning over to one side on that little training wheel, is not learning to ride a bike. That's a trike, unfortunately.

Learning to ride an awkward, lopsided bike/trike object is no simple matter. In fact, it's pretty difficult for little kids to pedal a bike while steering it, especially if it's flopped over onto a tiny wheel. Because of the difficulty of pedaling and steering at the same time, only bigger kids are able to use training wheel–equipped pedal bikes successfully. And since training wheels, again, don't really teach kids to ride bikes, American kids in the twentieth century usually didn't master two-wheelers until they were 5 or 6 years old.

In the age of the balance bike, that sounds crazy. Our 2-year-old coasted down a hill on her balance bike, feet up, on her first day with the bike! See, balance bikes are magic. Your work is done here.

It remains to be seen what, if any, profound long-term effects will result from having an entire generation of toddlers learn to ride bikes before they can speak coherently. With a three- or four-year head start on the kids of yesteryear, today's munchkins are sure to develop more skill on two wheels. Since skilled riders often perform riskier actions, it's unclear if that skill will translate into safer riding. But we can say this: By the time they're ready to navigate the wide world on their own, or almost on their own as the case may be, they'll be able to concentrate fully on the task at hand without struggling with the bike itself. Maybe they'll be more likely to grow into avid riders or car-free parents themselves, creating a bike-loving culture that sweeps the nation. Certainly they'll have a lot more fun as two-wheeled toddlers than we did on our trikes and Bigwheels. Although, admittedly, Bigwheels were awesome.

The New Paradigm

The balance bike really is a shrunken version of the pre-bicycle "running machine," invented by Baron Karl von Drais in 1816. Little did they know in the early 1800s that the running machine would be resurrected and miniaturized to serve as sensible transportation for toddlers 200 years later.

Balance bikes teach kids to ride, but that's only part of the story. More importantly, kids love them! Love them! Toddlers bubble over with joy at the mere thought of riding their own bikes. When they actually see a balance bike being used by another kid, they freak out. Then, when they finally straddle their very own toddler-size bikes and start scooting around, they become almost drunk with happiness. If your kid doesn't seem to love the idea of riding a balance bike, don't push it. Find another activity and maybe they'll come around to the two-wheeler in a month, a year. If not, that's fine too.

The best way to teach a kid to ride a balance bike is to let her watch another kid who has it down already. If properly fascinated by the display of prowess, your child will want to imitate it immediately and will climb on her own balance bike and start gliding around after a few tries. We have a disagreement about this, however. One of us (Robert) thinks parents should avoid holding up the child and bike, or pushing her along, or any of that. He thinks that's as likely to stall the progression as it is to help. After all, the whole point of the balance bike is that kids riding them won't fall over if they lose their balance, they just put their feet down. They don't need anybody to hold them up. The other one (Christie) thinks that's pretty silly, and says that toddlers might need a little extra help when they're just starting to figure out a balance bike.

Toddlers can still crash balance bikes, you will find out. Usually when they get rolling downhill for the first time. They start wobbling then auger into the ground, kind of like out-of-control mountain bikers. They can land right on the protruding handlebar, and there is even some potential for painful injuries as a result. We think toddlers need to wear crash helmets when riding balance bikes. Helmets are probably as important for balance bikers as they are for older kids. (See the "Kids' Helmets" chapter.) Other kinds of protective gear shouldn't be necessary.

Once they learn how to glide, balance bikers are cyclists, facing some of the same potential wrecks so cherished and enjoyed by adult riders. Are balance bikes dangerous? Well, they do start with B . . . and that rhymes with T . . . and that stands for Trouble. Seriously, tales of carnage and woe associated with balance bikes are pretty scarce. Considering how popular they are, it seems like circumstantial evidence is strongly in favor of the notion that balance bikes are generally safe. But there will most likely be some awkward tumbles and frights and frustration, especially in those first few tries.

If at all possible, let the kid become acquainted with the balance bike on a softer surface before moving to concrete or asphalt. But keep in mind that it's much harder for a kid to scoot the bike along through grass, so it could be more frustrating to learn on a surface like that. Shallow grass-covered slopes are great for learning to glide, with gravity helping. Narrow sidewalks lined with soft grass make pretty good runways for early riders. It gives them a smooth surface for easy rolling, and if they fall over there's a decent chance they'll land on the grass.

It's a lot harder to crash or fall over if the seat's so low that the child can stand on the ground while straddling the seat. If she starts to lose it, she can almost always just stick a leg out. The very dangerous exception is when the child gets good at gliding, and gets rolling down a hill faster than she can control. At that point some sort of crash is almost inevitable, and it's going to be bad.

To illustrate just how dangerous balance bikes tend not to be, consider the fun game our daughter developed during her first week with her balance bike. Rolling along happily, she'd turn to us and say, "I might fall down. I might fall down." Okay, we'd say. Be careful. Then she'd stop and very dramatically lay the bike over and sit on it, making mock distress noises, "Oh no, I falled down!" Rolling along without incident was getting too predictable and she wanted to spice things up a bit! She was a little disappointed at first with the balance bike's crash-and-burn potential. Before too long, she would get more than she bargained for.

One of the things that concerned us (or, at least, Robert) about balance bikes was the fact that the whole system relies on toddlers supporting their weight on the seats while gliding along. On a normal bike with pedals, you can (and should) distribute your body weight to five contact points: the rear end, two hands, and two feet. Without pedals, there's really only one place to put the weight if the feet are off the ground—crotch city. Toddlers can deal with that kind of thing very well, but should they? Was this a potentially damaging feature of balance bikes? We wondered. But other parents didn't seem to be thinking about anything like that, and the kids didn't seem to mind at all. "If the kid is starting to feel discomfort, he will just put his feet on the ground," said one parent.

There isn't much else to be concerned about here. Obviously you'll want to make sure your kid doesn't go cruising into traffic on a balance bike. If they're gliding around the driveway or sidewalk in front of the house, stay present to ensure they don't decide to roll off somewhere. Set definite boundaries about where and how they can ride. Pay particular attention to any slope on which the child could gain too much speed. Then sit back and watch while your kid has the time of her life and learns to ride a bike without your having to teach her.

Spreading the joy of bicycling to a new generation, balance bikes are a huge gift to humanity and to children.

Is My Child Old Enough for a Balance Bike?

Is my child old enough? It's not a question that was heard often during the tricycles-and-training wheels era.

We think the minimum safe age for balance biking is determined by the child's ability to walk. Just being able to walk isn't really enough. The child should be able to walk very well, and run, and have all sorts of movement mastered before trying a balance bike. If they're still in that stage where they fall down seemingly at random, they're not ready. To get the most out of a balance bike, a child should be able to pick it up off the ground, swing a leg over the frame while holding it up, then do the reverse when it's time to do something else. The child should also be adept at falling over when it happens, meaning he should be good at getting his hands out to soften a fall, a learned skill. Not that balance biking involves a whole lot of falling over—it doesn't. That's kind of the whole point.

Of course all kids develop at different rates, but it seems like the second birthday would be a fine time to introduce a toddler to her first balance bike, provided the bike is small enough to be safely ridden by such a youngster (don't torture your kid with a new balance bike that is too large to ride). Eighteen months is pushing it, but we've certainly heard of a lot of children who were starting to two-wheel by then. By two and a half, almost all kids will be ready to try it.

The most important thing is the child's enthusiasm. If she's not excited by the mere sight of a cool balance bike, and begging you to let her try, it might not be good to push her into it.

Buyer's Guide

This category will make your head spin. There are a gazillion different balance bikes available these days. There are so many different brands that several of them have very similar names and are easily confused, perhaps by design.

We actually pared down this list a considerable amount, so it's far from comprehensive. Listing all the balance bikes for sale would require a book in itself. These aren't all necessarily great products listed below, but the selection is a pretty fair representation of what kind of balance bikes are available, from basic and budget-friendly to unusual and unaffordable.

Expect to spend about a hundred bucks, give or take a twenty, for a decent balance bike from a respected manufacturer. Expect to spend *at least* $50 more for some snazzy Euro stuff that will score points at the artisanal cider stand. There are lots of deals online, though, and even a thriving used market. (Which means you'll probably be able to unload your used balance bike some day without much hassle.)

There are cheaper balance bikes available at "big box" stores for $40 or so. They look like the more expensive bikes, but their lower quality becomes apparent in the details, immediately after purchase and over time. Buyers are attracted to the idea of buying a fully assembled bike, which they may be able find at one of these stores. But we'd rather leave assembly to the parents or a competent bike shop. We left them off the list.

If you get a new balance bike, chances are it comes to your house in a box from a distant location (China). Don't fret; assembly is quite simple and all the necessary tools should be included in the package. Some balance bikes (the Burley MyKick, for instance) come almost fully assembled in the box.

When you get right down to it, all balance bikes are pretty basic. It's amazing how simple bikes become when the drivetrains are removed. Frame/fork, wheels and tires, a seat and seat post, and a handlebar with stem and grips. That's all she wrote. (Oh, and the optional brake.)

Honestly, as much as we love supporting the local bike shops, you don't need one for this. This is a natural online purchase.

What Size?

Balance bikes vary a surprising amount in size and adjustability. This adds an unwelcome layer of complexity for parents who don't want to think too much about the purchase.

The bike's seat height range is probably the first and most important variable to look at before buying, because there is a danger of buying a bike that your child can't even ride. Some of the models have a fairly large height range, while others have a very tight range. Unfortunately you can't assume that any bike will fit any toddler. It will be tricky to find one single balance bike that will fit your child throughout her balance biking years. Kids grow into them and then out of them.

If a manufacturer provides only a recommended age for their product, ignore it. It's an almost meaningless number.

Note that some manufacturers list minimum inseam length needed to use their products, while others list minimum seat height. These are not the same things! The balance bike's seat will have to be an inch or so lower than the child's crotch when the child is standing up straight. Measure the child's inseam then subtract an inch to approximate the ideal seat height. Note that this is a different sort of calculation than we use for a pedal bike, a different kind of machine. On a pedal bike a child might not be able to quite touch the ground while sitting straight up on the seat, but they'll be able to if they lean the bike over a little bit or stand over the bike in front of the seat. "Standover height" (the distance between the ground and the bike's top tube) is a more important measure on a pedal bike.

Obviously you want something that not only fits your kid now, but fits for some time into the future as well. Ideally your child's perfect seat height is right near the minimum of her new bike's range. Worst-case scenario, you get one that's already too small for your kid. Ack! Happens all the time unfortunately. Getting a too-large bike is less disastrous, but may not seem so to your child, if she's been anxious to ride it then finds out she can't. Serious drama.

Weight

Toddlers' balance bikes tend to weigh between 7 and 11 pounds. You shouldn't choose a balance bike based on its light weight, but you might just decide to forego a certain model if its weight is much over 11 pounds. Extra-heavy balance bikes are noticeably more difficult for little kids to handle. Beyond that, if a manufacturer can't keep the weight of the bike in a normal range, it's a red flag.

Wheels and Tires

Some balance bikes have little spoked wheels with pneumatic tires, just like the big kid bikes. Many others sport tires made of "solid foam rubber" (ethylene vinyl acetate, aka EVA). The solid tires don't get flats, but they don't perform as well either. They're more likely to slide out, especially on dirt and gravel, and may not provide as smooth a ride for your munchkin. They also disintegrate over time.

Solid tires are especially tempting in areas where bicyclists experience an inordinate amount of punctures—the dry, goathead-infested areas of the western United States come to mind. Truthfully, however, a thick enough tire tread, the likes of which appear on many balance bike tires, will prevent thorn flats due to thickness alone. If you think your rug rat will be riding the bike on dirt, pneumatic tires will be important to have. Air-filled tires perform better on all surfaces, but the difference is obvious on the rough stuff. Solid tires are just easier and a little cheaper.

Of course not all pneumatic tires are created equal. Very low-quality pneumatics are often spec'd on the cheaper balance bikes, and these are known to fall apart with alarming rapidity. Your child doesn't need great tires, but you also don't want to have to deal with buying new tires a year or so down the line. That'll make you bitter. Balance bike tires don't have to be very durable to last through the useful life of the bike, even when it's handed down through multiple children. So when the tiny tires fall apart so quickly, as some parents report, it suggests that the manufacturer has decided to really push the cost savings, to the point that the safety of the rider becomes affected.

Most of the bikes listed below have 12-inch wheels (an approximate measure from tire edge to tire edge), but many balance bikes have 10-inch wheels. Any smaller than that and the wheels' inability to roll well over relatively minor obstacles becomes a pretty serious issue. A balance bike with sub-10-inch wheels is really an indoor machine.

Some balance bikes meant for taller, older kids come with 14- or even 16-inch tires. If your kid is tall enough to use one of these, however, you have to ask yourself if it makes more sense at that point to get a regular kids' pedal bike and take the drivetrain off. That could save you from having to buy another bike in a few months. It could also be the case that a child who fits onto a bike with 14-inch wheels has another year or two of pedal-less gliding to do.

One company, Early Rider, makes a balance bike with a fat 12-inch tire in back and a 14-inch tire in front. This is an interesting twist that could keep the bike usable for a longer period of time as the kid grows. It should also help smaller kids enjoy the benefits of a better-rolling big front wheel.

Steel spokes aren't devil-spawn, but they have been known to catch the occasional foot or hand. No barefoot balance bikers! A lot of balance bikes are equipped with plastic wheels with five big spokes. A few of the wooden models (Skuut and LIKEaBIKE) have solid disc wheels, which is marketed as a safety feature.

To Brake or Not to Brake

Should you get a balance bike with a brake? That is the question. Well, one of the questions.

Interesting question. Some balance bikes are equipped with a single hand brake attached to the rear wheel via a drum brake or V-brake (balance bikes obviously can't have coaster brakes, because they don't have pedals/chains/sprockets). We used to think that these brakes are installed primarily for the benefit of parents rather than kids. Parents expect to see brakes on bikes they buy for their kids, and can be alarmed when they're not there. Without having thought about it much, they assume that a brakeless balance bike must be cut-rate, low-performance, and dangerous.

Most balance bikes still have no brake at all. Don't be too alarmed. If you cringe when you think of your toddler trying to stop without a brake, imagine her attempt to stop being dependent on a brake that doesn't function very well and a brake lever that she can barely reach. The brake adds a layer of complexity to the whole thing; your child will have to learn past it. Safety-wise, it could (maybe) do more harm than good, at least initially. Most parents find that their toddlers do just fine without any brake—or rather, by using their shoes as brakes, Fred Flintstone–style. That's usually the plan with balance bikes, and it works. Usually.

It is also true, however, that toddlers who know how to use hand brakes will have more tools at their disposal—shoes plus hand brake—and should be able to stop more efficiently than the brakeless toddler down the street. This won't seem necessary at first, but give 'em a few weeks or months with the bike and suddenly they're zooming around so well that stopping power becomes a much more serious issue. And if they're going to progress from the balance bike to a regular bike, there's a good chance that the new bike will have hand brakes too, so maybe that early practice will have benefits later on. (The balance bike's brake is probably going to be attached to the rear wheel, though, so the kid will still have to learn all about front wheel braking when he gets that new bike.)

We could take this brake argument one step further and mention that a good brake will allow your child to go faster than she could without. Do you want your child to go faster? If a toddler is cruising around fast enough on a balance bike that a hand brake becomes necessary, that's a bit faster than the intended balance bike experience.

Personally, we're believers in brakes on balance bikes. Our kid turned us into believers. She got really good at gliding on a brakeless balance bike, and all was going well. The presence of a moderate hill on our street, however, became a pretty serious issue. One day, after several successful runs down the hill, using her feet alone to check her speed, she got a little overconfident at the top and really charged down the thing. Well, she got going so fast that she outran her ability to slow down using her feet. She also outran her parents' ability to catch up using their feet! This scenario can only end in disaster of some sort. She lost control and crashed pretty hard—way harder than a 2-year-old should be crashing a bike. It was bad, but not nearly as bad as it could have been had she smacked straight into some object, or rolled into the intersection at the bottom of the block. Suddenly, a brake made a huge amount of sense.

If you get a bike with a brake, make sure you try it with your own hand before giving the bike to the kid. A good percentage of these balance bike brakes barely function. Make sure the lever can be pulled by a toddler's hand, first of all, then make sure it actually does something. If it's really weak and seems worthless, fix it before letting your kid ride the bike. If it can't be fixed (a decent possibility with low-quality machines), you may as well remove it.

Either way, brake or no brake, you and your kid will adapt and make it work!

Other Features

Increasingly, balance bikes have steering limiters, rudimentary devices that keep the handlebars from turning too far in either direction. Steering limiters will prevent some "jackknife"-style crashes, which sounds good to parents, but in reality the kid will be fine without a steering limiter, and will crash anyway with a steering limiter. The classic wooden balance bikes feature limited steering as a natural consequence of their front-end design.

Quick release seat post clamps are pretty cool on balance bikes, but not that important. "No-tools adjustment" could save you a little hassle when you're dialing in the kid's optimal seat height. How much we should be willing to pay for that is another issue. Not much, we say. Many of the more affordable metal-framed bikes have quick release seat posts, while many do not. (Wooden balance bikes can't have no-tools adjustment, due to their design.)

Seat style and quality varies widely on balance bikes. Some balance bikes have nice, cushy seats. Some, like the cheaper Strider, have plastic seats with virtually no padding. That's not necessarily a horrible thing, but considering the peculiar ergonomics of the "running machine," we think it's better for the seat to have a little padding.

You will probably come to appreciate the rubber bumpers at the end of the handlebar grips, if your kid's bike has them. If it doesn't, you may wish it did. The extra rubber protects the bike as well as the surfaces upon which it gets repeatedly and unceremoniously dumped. Toddlers have no respect for flooring.

Higher-end models also have recessed bolts, whereas the cheap ones have exposed bolts. Exposed bolts aren't the end of the world, but Allen bolts are easier to deal with.

Footrests? Most balance bikes are without any sort of footrests. Your toddler won't miss not having them. In fact, because they make the bike a little wider, they could hinder a young-un's ability to scoot on the bike a little bit. Later on, when your child has mastered the balance bike but hasn't yet moved on to a pedal bike, built-in footrests might help her squeeze some more mileage out of the balance bike.

Invasion of the Wooden Frames

Wooden balance bikes have taken this market by storm. Styled to appeal to parents as much as kids, these whimsical machines can be as sturdy as their steel-framed cousins, while looking like something cobbled together by elves. Buyers of wooden balance bikes are in danger of being snookered by style and packaging, no doubt about it. The manufacturers see your Etsy self coming a mile away. Some companies are trying to capitalize on the hot trend by selling really junky products that look like the higher-quality wooden balance bikes. We tried to leave those fakers off the list. But there are some really cool offerings among the superficial glitz, with prices grounded more in high quality than greed.

Unlike some bargain basement knock-offs, good-quality wooden balance bike frames are made with laminated marine-quality plywood and are quite resistant to the elements—you can pretty much leave them out in the rain without worrying that they're going to be ruined, for instance. But they do show wear. They get nicked up. Metal frames get battle-scarred too—you won't find multi-layer, super-durable paint jobs on sub-$200 balance bikes—but nothing like the wooden frames. And consequently you can expect a new wooden balance bike to look very used before too long. A rig that shows wear is better than a rig that stays shiny and fresh because it never leaves the house, though.

Seat height adjustment is about the only other major difference between the wooden and metal balance bikes. While steel-framed bikes have traditional seat posts and clamps, which can be set anywhere in the post's workable range, seats on a wooden bike can only be placed at pre-set heights.

Usually only four possible positions are available to set a wooden seat pillar. In addition, changing the seat height on wooden balance bikes requires the removal of bolts, while adjustment of traditional seat posts is a bit easier, even without a quick release lever.

LIKEaBIKE is a popular favorite among the wooden bikes, but their prices are ahead of the pack, in the $300 range. Used LIKEaBIKEs can be good finds. Early Rider makes durable, high-quality wooden machines as well, and they sell for about a hundred dollars less. Cheaper still are the Skuut and Prince Lionheart, with the same basic look as the others, but with noticeably lower quality. There are a lot of complaints online from buyers of these two models, after their budget bikes broke in garden-variety toddler tumbles. Any cheaper than that and you're into pretty sketchy territory.

Metal and Composite Frames

Among the metal-framed bikes, Strider is a flagship brand selling relatively affordable little bikes of acceptable quality. Most of the comparison shopping seems to invoke the Strider. It is the standard by which other balance bikes are judged. Upstart companies base their entire spiel on "better than Strider." We list two of their models below, but if you want to spend a bit more you can get a lighter aluminum "high-performance" Strider—maybe Junior is training for the toddler pentathlon—or one that has motorsport-themed stickers.

The Radio Flyer is a solid choice in the sub-$100 range, but may not be suitable for shorter/younger riders (check that seat height range).

The Burley MyKick is a steel balance bike with some different features. It's the only bike we're aware of that has "honeycombed" foam rubber tires with air pockets inside, to give better performance and a smoother ride while remaining flat-free. It also has a padded seat and ball-bearing hubs and headset, basic features often missing on similarly priced bikes. The Verde Scout and Tykebykes 12 are

The Burley MyKick has unique tires, airless but honeycombed for better ride quality. *Courtesy Burley*

both metal-framed bikes, similar to the Burley in price and quality, but both are lighter than the Burley.

Miir is a Seattle water bottle company that started selling bikes a few years ago. Their Bambini balance bike, which has been selling at REI, is a very basic, light, steel-framed balance bike with a twist for soft-hearted souls—"For every Miir Bambini purchased, a second bike is provided to someone in need." Miir has joined forces with organizations that provide bicycles to low income people in Africa and to the poor in American cities like Boise and Seattle.[1]

FirstBIKE is an exception to the endless parade of very similar looking wooden and steel balance bikes. The FirstBIKEs have flashy-looking fiberglass composite frames. This doesn't cut down the weight all that much, if you're wondering, but it does mean the frame is weatherproof, and generally more durable than wood. (Also "insect proof" according to one retailer.)[2] If your child's last balance bike was consumed by termites, maybe this is the bike for you. Flexing of the composite frame could become an issue for heavier, older kids. The composite FirstBIKE is in the same price range as most of the other balance bikes.

If you really want to go nuts, you can buy your toddler a carbon fiber, high-performance balance bike by Zelvy. Price is about $1,000. So not too bad. Go for it. Get two.

Product List

Burley MyKick. $129. Steel frame. 12.5-inch "honeycombed" foam rubber tires. Spoked wheels. Seat height: 12.5–16 inches. Padded seat. No-tools seat height adjustment.

Diggin Active Skuut. $79. Wood frame. 12-inch pneumatic tires. Seat height: 13.5–16.5 inches.

Early Rider Classic 12/14. $180. Wood frame. 12-inch pneumatic FatBoy rear tire, 14-inch pneumatic front tire. Spoked wheels. Seat height: 13–15.3 inches. Recessed bolts.

Early Rider Lite 12. $160. 12.5-inch pneumatic Kenda FatBoy tires. Seat height: 11.6–15 inches. About 7 pounds.

FirstBIKE Street. $159. Fiberglass composite frame. 12-inch pneumatic Schwalbe tires. Seat height: 13.7–17.8 inches. (Optional "lowering kit" lowers seat height range to 12–16 inches.) Tool-free seat height adjustment. Optional hand brake. Also available in "Cross" model with knobby tires and hand brake, and "Racing" model with Schwalbe Big Apple tires and hand brake.

The FirstBIKE has a unique design among balance bikes. *Courtesy FIRSTBike*

Islabikes Rothan. $189, not including shipping. Aluminum frame. 12-inch pneumatic tires. Seat height: 11.5–16 inches (11.5–18 inches with optional long seat post). V-brake.

The Islabikes Rothan weighs in at 7.7 pounds with its aluminum frame, special toddler-size hand brake, and pneumatic tires. *Courtesy Islabikes*

Janod Vanilla Scooter. $109. 10-inch pneumatic tires. Unique style. Looks just like a little Vespa. Works well for very young or small toddlers.

Kinderbike Laufrad. $119. Aluminum frame. 12-inch pneumatic tires. Spoked wheels. V-brake. Seat height: 13–18.5 inches. Tool-free seat height adjustment. Padded seat. Includes bell.

One of the smallest balance bikes available, the Kinderbike E-Series has a tiny steel frame and a choice of pneumatic tires on alloy rims or airless on plastic rims. *Courtesy Kinderbike*

Kinderbike Laufrad Mini. $119. Aluminum frame. 12-inch pneumatic tires. Spoked wheels. V-brake. Seat height: 11–16.5 inches. Tool-free seat height adjustment. Padded seat. Includes bell.

LIKEaBIKE Forest. $330. Wood frame. 12-inch pneumatic knobby tires. Solid disc wheels. Seat height: 12.5–16.1 inches.

LIKEaBIKE Jumper. $300. Aluminum frame with rear suspension. 12-inch pneumatic tires. Spoked wheels. Seat height: 14.4–18.5 inches. No-tools seat height adjustment. Padded seat.

LIKEaBIKE Mini. $315. Wood frame. 12-inch pneumatic knobby tires. Solid disc wheels. Seat height: 9.8–13.4 inches. One of the smallest balance bikes available.

Miir Bambini. $139. Steel frame. 12-inch foam rubber tires. Seat height: 15–18.5 inches. Quick release seat post.

Muna. $109. 12-inch pneumatic tires. Steel frame. Seat height: 13–18 inches. Drum brake. Relatively heavy at 12 pounds. South African company.

Novara Zipper. $100. Steel frame. 12-inch foam rubber tires. Seat height: 17.25–19 inches. Available in "boys' and girls' colors." With a minimum seat height of 17.25 inches, this is a tall bike, not suitable for young toddlers or short kids.

Radio Flyer Glide & Go. $65. Steel frame. 12-inch foam rubber tires. Seat height: 14.5–18 inches. Includes bell.

Spawn Cycles Tengu. $235. Aluminum frame. 12-inch pneumatic tires. V-brake. Seat height: 11.5–16.5 inches.

Specialized Hotwalk. $175. Aluminum frame. 12-inch pneumatic tires. Spoked wheels. Padded seat. Seat height: 13.5–17 inches.[3] The Hotwalk is available in boys' and girls' models. The girls' model has a "step through" frame.

Strider Classic. $100. Steel frame. 12-inch foam rubber tires. Seat height: 11–16 inches. Non-padded seat.

Strider Sport. $119. Steel frame. 12-inch foam rubber tires. Seat height: 11–19 inches. Padded seat. Handlebar pad. No-tools seat and handlebar adjustment.

TykeBykes 12. $109. Aluminum frame. 12-inch pneumatic tires. Spoked wheels. Seat height: 13–18 inches. Drum brake.

Verde Scout. $129. Aluminum frame. 12-inch pneumatic tires. Spoked wheels. Seat height: 14–16.5 inches. BMX pads and overall style. Very limited height range. This bike has a diamond frame rather than a step-through frame, and may be difficult for many kids to handle.

Vilano. $75. Steel frame. 12-inch foam rubber tires. Seat height: 15.5–17.5 inches.

Yedoo TooToo. $129. Steel frame. 12-inch pneumatic tires. Spoked wheels. Seat height: 13–18 inches. V-brake. Steering limiter. Czech company.

CHAPTER 15

Kids' Bikes

Too Young to Pedal?

It's not a question that our parents ever had to think about. By the time we were finally overcoming our training wheels, we were far older—and our brains were more developed—than the toddlers learning to ride two-wheelers today. We were more than ready for pedal bikes; today's little balancers may need a year or two of "stalling" before they go to the next phase.

Pedal bikes are different than balance bikes, and not just because they have pedals. Balance bikes only need to provide enough clearance for the seat post at its lowest point, and can be very close to the ground. Pedal bikes must provide ample clearance for the pedals, so they don't strike the ground with each stroke or when the bike is leaned over. Consequently, pedal bike frames and riders are higher off the ground.

On a pedal bike the child can ride even if she is too short to reach the ground while sitting on the seat, though it isn't a great idea to try this before the kid knows how to compensate for the height of the bike by leaning it over or stepping in front of the seat when she needs to reach the ground. The child may be a great little pedaler, cruising all over the place, but might not be able to stop and get off the bike without falling over. Some toddlers can

Pedal bikes might give some little kids more freedom than they can handle.
shironosov/iStock/Thinkstock

pedal and balance just fine, having graduated quickly from balance bikes, but their parents have to run along next to them to grab them when they want to stop pedaling. You don't want to get caught in that loop.

The balance bike phenomenon has put parents in an awkward position. We're right there too. Our 2-year-old took to the balance bike and was gliding along within days. It's pretty obvious that she could transition to pedaling almost seamlessly. But she's not even two and a half, and she's not ready yet. Not even close. Sure, she could pedal a tiny bike, but what's the point? To make a cute video, one-up the other parents at the park whose kids are still on tricycles? Where's she going to go on that thing? We wouldn't be able to ride with her in any safe manner. Even the bike paths would be too much for us. She certainly wouldn't be able to go off anywhere by herself—and she would want to. We live on a busy street and don't really have any sort of enclosed area for her to cruise safely within. All in all, it's a recipe for heartache.

So we don't want to introduce her to a pedal bike yet. We'll stick to the balance bike, maybe even get her a newer, fancier one—with a brake—and

Bea can really get rolling on her LIKEaBIKE Forest and enjoys off-roading with her knobby tires. *Robert Hurst*

will thus be able to continue cruising the sidewalks in a safe way, with Bea scooting and gliding while one of us walks (or jogs, as the case may be) along with her, making sure she stops at all alley intersections and doesn't roll into the street.

We're not sure when she'll be ready for that real bike. She'll have to develop a little more awareness of her surroundings, and demonstrate an ability to listen carefully to her parents and respond to directions. Stuff like that. Both Bea and her parents need more maturity before we try that. Judging by what other parents are dealing with, it seems like she'll be pedaling like a banshee before her fourth birthday. Then we'll have to work out some places where we can go to safely enjoy riding together.

Training Wheels?

Training wheels don't necessarily aid children in their journey toward balancing a two-wheeler. The learning process is sort of put on hold as the child pushes the training-wheeled rig around, as it does not perform much like a bicycle.

"But we all learned to ride just fine with training wheels," says middle-aged America.

Well, no, we didn't. We learned to ride *in spite of* training wheels. Kids these days learn to ride bikes several years earlier than we did, using a completely different, training wheel–less method: balance bikes, of course. (No, we do not own stock in a balance bike company, but that is a pretty good idea and we should look into it.)

Training wheels are obsolete as a way to teach kids to ride bikes. However, they may still be useful. Training wheels allow a small kid to climb onto and at least sit on a pedal bike, even if they're too small to pedal and steer it. That's great exercise for little pedalers. They may be able to push the pedals and move the bike around a little on their own, or parents may be tasked to push the child-and-bike around (making the bike a glorified version of the big plastic push toys in the back yard). It's not really a bike and won't teach the kid to ride one, but it's some kind of toy that might be fun. It could also be stupidly dangerous for such a low-speed endeavor; any kid who does this should be wearing a helmet.

As a general rule, don't buy a bike with training wheels for a child who has not yet learned to balance. At that size the child will be much happier and have a lot more fun on a balance bike, and will actually learn to ride. Later on, when transitioning to a pedal bike, it might help to use training wheels for a short transition period, and if the kid's already learned to balance, this shouldn't hurt his progress much.

Often a well-meaning grandparent or uncle, somebody who has yet to hear about the magic of balance bikes, will buy a toddler a tiny pedal bike with training wheels attached. The third birthday is when this commonly occurs. Don't chuck it off a tall building and tell your kid monsters stole it. Don't attach seventy-five helium balloons to it and set it aloft in the night. Instead consider making a balance bike out of it by lowering the seat all the way and removing the pedals, maybe the cranks and chain as well. This is where the unassembled reality of many cheap kids' bikes can actually be a boon. If the kid can reach the ground with his feet, that'll work just fine, at least temporarily. But that's a lot of extra hassle that parents don't need.

This is going to sound just plain mean and insensitive, but unannounced gifts of bicycles can really mess things up, especially when so many in the older generation(s) still have training wheels on the brain. The best course of action after receiving a 12-inch training wheel bike may be to exchange it for a balance bike.

Convertible Bikes

Some little kids' bikes are explicitly designed to convert from balance bikes to regular pedal bikes. Seemingly this is the perfect solution for parents who don't want to buy two or more bikes as their child progresses to pedals. The convertible bikes unfortunately have some troubling flaws ingrained. Beyond that the idea has been poorly executed by the industry, although as this book goes to press, there are some more promising bikes becoming available.

Fundamentally it is difficult to combine a balance bike and a pedal bike because they are, paradoxically, such different machines. The balance bike's seat needs to be close to the ground for the concept to work; the pedal bike, on the other hand, needs to have enough clearance for pedals and cranks, while providing an ergonomically acceptable pedaling position for the child.

Practically speaking, manufacturers seem to have done a poor job solving that fundamental riddle and combining the two types of bikes, if the intensity of Internet complaining is any indication. In some cases convertible bikes are so poorly designed that riding them is very difficult. On any kids' bike, but particularly on convertible bikes, pay attention to the horizontal distance between the pedals, a variable known in bike-speak as the Q-factor. Makers of convertible bikes have had trouble keeping the Q-factor within an ergonomically acceptable distance for kids—or have simply forgotten about it entirely.

There have been rumors and rumblings in the bike industry about some better quality convertible bikes coming onto the market. If you're interested, check for yourself, but they don't seem to be here just yet.

Weight

Kids' bikes weigh a ton, usually. It's not fair. Kids are victimized in this game, caught between shady profit-seekers and clueless parents. The manufacturers sell comically hefty kids' bikes because they're much cheaper to make; parents buy them because they don't know any better. So kids are out there busting their guts trying to move bikes that are heavier than the bikes their dads ride. It's completely absurd.

People are kidding themselves if they think kids don't care how much their bikes weigh. It's a comforting thought. But let a kid who has been riding a typical tank try an appropriately light bike, then see which one they prefer.

What Size?

For your kid's first pedal bike, look for a bike with 14- or 16-inch wheels/tires. Twelve-inch pedal bikes may work under special circumstances. Many parents out there are looking for a solution to the desire for a pedal bike of their too-small toddler. Our daughter, just a few weeks after starting on the balance bike, was pointing at bigger kids' bikes and noting, "He has pedals!" Uh oh, we thought. But then she would start gliding around on her balance bike, having a great time, and the pedals were forgotten.

Twelve-inch pedal bikes may be problematic for a few reasons. The geometry and riding position are often all messed up. Not that a small child needs a super-efficient riding position, but it would be nice if it were remotely in the right ballpark. And the child is likely to grow out of a 12-inch pedal bike very quickly. If you can get your kid to forget about pedals for just a little bit longer, you should be able to avoid buying an ephemeral 12-inch bike and skip right to the 14-incher.

If a child is too small for a 14-inch, she may not be ready for all the different things that come along with riding a pedal bike. The freedom of a pedal bike requires responsibility. Yes, responsibility! A little bit, anyway. Even when ridden in an enclosed area, pedals give the child a great deal more freedom than she had with a balance bike. Now she can get going way too fast at just about any time she chooses.

There is extra responsibility not just in riding a pedal bike but in purchasing one too. Just what you wanted to hear. Ideally, for instance, you should take your child to the bike shop before purchasing the bike, to make sure the thing fits and will remain in the right size range for at least a little while. Make sure her tiny hand can reach and pull the brake lever without difficulty. Then try to give the kid a choice between a few different suitable bikes so they feel invested in the decision.

As with balance bikes, there is quite a bit of variation in size among the different brands, so there is that nagging possibility of buying a bike that doesn't fit. Unlike balance bikes, the sizing of small pedal bikes is often difficult to derive from the information provided by manufacturers online. To save money in the long run, find a 16-inch bike that is just small enough to work but has plenty of room for adjustment as the child grows. Of course it doesn't always work out so neatly.

Buyers, especially Internet shoppers, will want to measure the child's inseam; this measurement is not quite as critical as it was during the balance bike phase but will give you some clues about which bikes are too large or small.

Hot tip: The seats on some 14-inchers, like the Islabikes Cnoc, can be dropped a bit lower than their stated minimum heights by swapping out the seat posts for one-piece BMX-style posts with attached seats.

The Islabikes Cnoc 14 is a serious rig! In the United States the Cnoc is sold with a rear coaster brake as required by law. Possibly named for a mountain in Scotland. *Courtesy Islabikes*

Brakes

In the United States, brakes on kids' bikes are found in two basic configurations: rear coaster brake with front hand brake, or rear coaster brake and no front brake. The Consumer Product Safety Commission disallows the sale of kids' bikes (small balance bikes being an exception) without coaster brakes in the United States. Curiously, the CPSC is just fine with kids' bikes that only have a coaster brake, without any front brake whatsoever. This may not be the smartest move for kids' safety, but kids make it work nonetheless.[1]

We like the idea of starting your kid on a front hand brake at this time, but it's not a requirement. Many a safe mile has been ridden with coaster brakes alone. The coaster brake is unlikely to need any maintenance, which is good, because you are unlikely to give it any if it does. Cheap V-brakes are probably going to sap more of your time.

One thing the coaster brake's not going to do is flip your kid over the handlebars. The child's first serious encounter with a front V-brake could very well have that result. But it makes sense to let the child learn about front brake modulation and body control sooner rather than later.

Before sending your child off to ride with a front brake for the first time, try to show him the basics of front wheel braking. Demonstrate, using your own bike if it's around, how a rider must move the body backward as pressure on the front brake is increased. He probably won't absorb the information until he feels it himself, but take a shot anyway.

Style

Style is starting to become a pretty huge factor by this point in your kid's life. It's time for parents to let their kids decide what kind of style they like, but there are a lot of pitfalls associated with that when bike shopping. Kids will demand bikes you can't afford, or bikes of lower quality than you want them to ride, or bikes that plain won't work for them, based on style alone.

Imagine yourself standing with your child in the local bike shop. You're going to buy your toddler her first pedal bike and have the purchase all worked out, but she points longingly at the 20-inch cruiser with the flower paint job. She won't be able to ride the thing for five years or so, but that matters little to her. She wants that paint job. She wants that bike.

BOB'S FIRST BIKE

My brother and I both learned to ride on a dark red mini Schwinn cruiser with red-and-white streamer tassel things coming out of the grips. It was perfect, but since that bike belonged to both of us, that bike belonged to neither of us.

Later my brother got a Schwinn Sting-Ray, with the banana seat and "ape-hanger" bars. The 900-pound Sting-Ray was okay, but by then BMX bikes were available, and I was more attracted to those beauties. Truthfully, I wanted a 50 cc Honda motorbike. But I knew that wasn't in the cards.

Unfortunately I didn't get a motorcycle or BMX bike. I ended up with a super-low-quality bike—pale yellow with black stripes—from a discount store called Duckwall's. I remember the stays and rear dropouts were sort of pinched together instead of welded, like a swing set. Every pedal stroke twisted the frame and caused loud cracking noises. It was a piece of junk.

But it was still a bike. I really started to fly around on that thing. I learned to pop wheelies up and down the block and worked the coaster brake into wicked power slides at every opportunity. I even had my first taste of dirt riding on that bike. The exhilaration of sweeping around a downhill turn on a singletrack trail for the first time is etched in my memory. I also remember a few

You don't buy her the huge flower bike, obviously, but it does mess up the program if she's not completely excited about the appropriately sized bike you do buy. It pays to surf the child's stylistic preferences as much as possible without giving in to every little whim. At that point you might be able to reach some sort of compromise to keep her excitement level high and your sanity level hovering in the acceptable range. We hope, for your sake, that there is! Ah, the art of parenting.

Reflective Materials

The CPSC requires side reflectors, front and rear reflectors, and pedal reflectors on all bikes besides "sidewalk bicycles," which are again exempt. Side reflectors can be in the form of reflective sidewalls or rims instead of traditional reflectors in the spokes.

spectacular and painful crashes. We became very close, that bike and I. Sometimes too close.

I rode that yellow hooptie into the ground. In the process I developed a love for riding bikes that continues today.

Riding one of the junkier bikes on the planet could not kill my childhood love for biking. On the other hand, maybe riding that creaky yellow junker cheated me out of an even greater joy that I might have felt on a better machine, a bike that would have loved to be ridden as much as I loved to ride it. I craved performance—and I understood very well that my cheap bike wasn't built for it. I knew I was pushing it past where it was meant to go. But I also knew that my parents didn't have a lot of money to throw around on fancy bikes, and at 10 years old or so I wasn't ready to go work in the mines.

As a parent now myself, father to a child who shows every indication of loving bikes even harder than her parents love bikes, I have a feeling we'll be shopping a lot more carefully for her first pedal bike than my parents did for mine. She's probably going to get hurt at some point on her new bike, but I don't want her to get hurt because of the bike itself. And if she's got the love like I did (and do), I want her to have a really fun bike to make the most of it.

You should add reflective material to a bike that doesn't already have it. Put reflective tape or even lights on the spokes and frame. You can get creative with it. You'll get the most bang for your buck by putting the reflective stuff on the spokes.

Children's coats and helmets should also be festooned with lights or reflective strips. Any child-carrying bicycle or bicycle accessory should also be strapped with reflective tape if it's not factory installed, including trailers and child seats, *bakfiets* boxes, and so forth.

The only danger of using these visibility-enhancing measures is that the user will put too much faith in their effectiveness. The sad fact is we could put white phosphorous sparklers on our heads and some drivers would still fail to notice our glittering, floodlit selves right there in front of them. If the driver's head isn't even pointed the right direction, it won't matter how visible you are. Some drivers' eyes are so bad that it doesn't really matter where

CPSC'S REGULATION AND TESTING OF KIDS' BICYCLES

Federal regulation of bicycles, as a consumer product, is a work in progress. The current regulations and testing requirements are laid out in the Code of Federal Regulations, Title 16, Part 1512. (See Code of Federal Regulations, Title 16 [Commercial Practices], Part 1512 [Requirements for Bicycles].) The feds have their eyes on many aspects of the bike, including the sharpness of protrusions, the effectiveness of the brakes and reflectors, the strength of the fasteners and components, and the bike's general roadworthiness. Children's bikes—"sidewalk bicycles" in federal regulatory parlance—are subject to less stringent standards than adult bikes. The wheels and frames of "sidewalk bicycles," for instance, are exempt from the specific strength requirements that apply to bigger bicycles. (A bicycle is defined as a "sidewalk bicycle" if its seat is not more than 25 inches from the ground when placed in the highest position.)

There is supposed to be some testing involved with children's bikes, however. Consider, for instance, the Sidewalk Bicycle Proof Test: "Procedure. The bicycle shall be loaded with weights of 13.6 kg (30 lb.) on the seat surface and 4.5 kg (10 lb.) attached to the end of each handle grip for a total load of 22.7 kg (50 lb.). The bicycle shall be lifted a distance of 0.3 m (1.0 ft.) and dropped (while maintaining an upright position) three times onto a paved surface. Following this and with weight removed, it shall be allowed to fall in any configuration and attitude from an upright position to the paved surface three times on each side." Yup, you read that right. They strap some weights to it, lift it up a foot, and drop it. Three times. Then they take the weights off and let it fall over several more times.

The bike passes the test if nothing breaks. Feel free to laugh if you ever see an ad for a kids' bike that brags about the frame "exceeding CPSC standards." In all seriousness the test makes some sense, because there's no acceptable way to test-ride kids' bikes. Bigger bikes are subjected to bone-jarring test rides by adult riders.

Other tests involve applying force to various parts of the bike and watching what happens. The stem-to-fork clamp test is a good example of these strength tests: "The handlebar-fork assembly shall be subjected to a torque applied about the axis of the stem, and shall then be disassembled and examined for signs of structural damage including cracking, splitting, stripping of threads, bearing damage, and bulging of the stem and fork structures. The handlebar and handlebar stem components shall be inspected for visible signs of galling, gouging, and scoring not due to normal assembly and disassembly operations . . . *Criteria.* There shall be no visible movement between the stem and fork when a torque of 47+3, -0 N-m (35+2, -0 ft=lb) for bicycles and 20+3, -0 N-m (15+2, -0 ft=lb) for sidewalk bicycles is applied to the handlebar about the stem-to-fork axis. There shall be no visible signs of damage to the stem-to-fork assembly or any component part thereof."

Other tests involve the brakes' ability to stop the bike. The requirement for adult bikes, to effect a full stop in 15 feet or less from 15 miles per hour, is quite easy to achieve. For kids' bikes the test involves simply clamping the brake and making sure it holds the wheel without any movement in the brake mechanism. The brakes don't have to be very strong, but they do have to do something.

Beyond that the CPSC spends a lot of energy on reflectors, reflectivity requirements, and testing of reflectivity.

Note: If you buy a bike, it hasn't been subjected to these drop or strength tests (thankfully). Not every bicycle that rolls off the assembly line is supposed to be tested like this. Manufacturers will test representative bikes in every production run, and any bike being sold in the United States should be able to pass these tests if randomly picked for testing by inspectors.

they are pointed. Keeping this sobering reality in mind, while lighting yourself and your child like a Trump high-rise nonetheless, is the winning combination. Assuming that all drivers will look toward you or notice you could be a very costly mistake.

Buyer's Guide

We've seen enough alarming stuff in the bike section at "big box" stores that we're going to avoid recommending any really cheap pedal bikes. So many companies that sell bikes seem to have put zero thought into designing bikes for kids. Many of the bikes created for the cheapo market thoughtlessly put little riders into some very awkward ergonomic positions—bad for pedaling, bad for handling. Other than keeping costs as low as possible, all these low-end manufacturers seem to care about is the style of the bike. The stickers. They view kids' bikes as mere toys. Combine bad design with the poor assembly that is so often found on these bikes and it's a real tragedy for kids.

The difference between the cheap 'Mart bikes and those that were thoughtfully designed for kids is huge! Unfortunately the price is pretty huge too.

It's interesting that so many of the nicer kids' bikes are made by foreign companies that specialize in kids' bikes. The big American brands, which one would think would know plenty about ergonomics and geometry in kids' bikes, have offered solid but heavy (relatively speaking) children's machines in the interest of keeping costs low. Their kids' bikes are boring, with piggish handling. They're not going to help light that fire for bicycling.

It's disappointing that a parent looking for a good bike for a kid has to dig up some obscure European or Canadian machine. There just haven't been enough of those discerning buyers in recent decades to make the big American bike companies give two hoots about the quality of their kids' bikes. If you think about it, this mindset has been part of the US bike industry since time began, and they've done very well with it. So why change? They may in the future, if they see those little companies really eating up their profits with high-quality juvenile bikes.

The Islabikes Cnoc 14 is one of these mysterious foreign models, an exceptional little high-performance machine, or at least it seems so relative to most little kids' bikes. At 12.4 pounds claimed weight, the difference is obvious. Many of the big brands' models weigh about twice as much. The bike also sports relatively aggressive geometry—steeper angles—which makes the steering much more responsive than typical kids' bikes. When riding this tiny BMX-style bike, the child will be leaning over more, with more weight over the front wheel. It might take some getting used to. One reviewer with a bike-happy tyke noted, "The first handful of rides were a bit nervous, and we had a few crashes that wouldn't have happened on a more upright frame, but the performance benefits made the memories of those skinned knees fade."[2] The author's use of the term "upright" refers to the body position of the rider. An "upright" bike actually has a laid-back frame. That is, the angle between the ground and the seat tube or head tube is more shallow. Performance bikes have bigger angles and really are more upright.

Islabikes is a UK company devoted to making high quality, thoughtfully designed bikes for kids. Fittingly, there aren't many retailers in the United States.

Early Rider offers a sleek looking—and relatively expensive—16-inch bike with a belt drive: highly unusual for a kids' bike, but could be very practical. Belt drives aren't as dangerous or dirty as chains, and require little if any maintenance (not that you'd be performing much maintenance on your kid's bike anyway, let's be honest). The bike, called the Belter, weighs in under 14 pounds, making it one of the lighter kids' bikes available. It looks like a miniature mountain bike racer and has a lower hand position than we usually find on little kids' bikes. We think the Belter's hand position is probably closer to ideal even for little kids. At $400, however, this silver streak will get little more than a chuckle and head shake from most parents.

Spawn is another of these foreign, kid-oriented bike companies. "When we went to find our son a 14-inch pedal bike we were faced with bikes that were heavier than him with training wheels, coaster brakes, huge chain guards and a bunch of other generally goofy things," write the people behind Canada's Spawn Cycles.[3] So they made a 14-pound bike with an aluminum frame, chromoly forks, and sealed bearings. Appropriately expensive at $385. With a bike called "Spawn," there is a good chance that you will be spending some time discussing the name with other parents, relatives, in-laws, and various neighborhood children. You may find this good or bad.

Dropping one price point, to around $200, the TykeBykes 16-inch pedal bike is a standout, with a cool chain case. (Chain cases are definitely not "goofy" on bikes for little kids, and as a parent you could really come to

BIKE RECALLS AND VIOLATIONS

In recent years numerous adult bicycles, from respected companies like Trek, BMC, Cannondale, Giant, and Specialized, have been recalled after failing catastrophically and causing injury to users. Many of the recalls involved high-end carbon frames and forks. There have been fewer recalls of children's bikes, and these recalls have affected low-end bikes, the kind you find at big box stores, almost exclusively. The following are some examples of recalls and violations in the children's bicycle industry within the past few decades.

Note: Just because a bicycle has been recalled doesn't mean the parents who purchased the bicycle will hear about the recall. Nobody is going to seek them out and give them the news. They may, by chance, hear of the CPSC's announcement and seek to redeem the manufacturer's offer, whatever it is. Most likely the vast majority of recalled products will never be repaired or replaced at the companies' expense. It seems to be a pretty forgiving course of action for the companies involved.

- On August 14, 2014, the CPSC ordered a halt to all sales of S-Frame 16-inch kids' bikes made by Hangzhou Wheelstar Cycle Company Limited of China, distributed in the United States by Ambica Imports, Inc. and sold mostly online. These cheapo bikes were found to have leaded paint. This was at least the third shipment of bikes made by the Hangzhou Wheelstar Cycle Company that was nailed for lead paint violation. The CPSC has seized hundreds of their products at the border.

- Over 3,000 20-inch "Turn N Burn" kids' bikes were recalled in the summer of 2014 after what the manufacturer said was a single report of a front wheel becoming detached from the forks. At $130, these bikes weren't cheap for toy store bikes.

appreciate it.) Trek and Specialized are there too, with pretty nice little bikes for the mass market. With them, you're going to be paying a little bit just for the names—for that sense of security. Diamondback has a very basic mini-BMX bike called the Mini Viper, at $160.

Customers were asked to contact Dynacraft for a free repair. (CPSC, "Dynacraft Recalls Avigo Youth Bicycles Due to Fall Hazard; Sold Exclusively at Toys "R" Us," July 31, 2014, Recall number 14-245.)

- After receiving thirteen reports of frames breaking on their MT220 girls' bicycles, and a handful of injuries that resulted, Trek and the CPSC recalled almost 50,000 bikes in 2008. The company offered customers a free replacement MT220 or a $100 discount on a different size Trek. (CPSC, "Trek Recalls Girls' Bicycles Due to Frame Failure," February 7, 2008, Release #08-186.)

- In 2007 Huffy recalled about 22,000 "Howler" and "Highland" bikes, sold at K-Mart stores, after a few people reported that the cranks popped off. Suddenly losing a crank can cause a serious crash, thus the recall. This is an example of poor assembly rather than shoddy manufacturing—exactly why so many people advise against buying a "Mart bike." Customers were not offered any replacement parts but were told to contact Huffy "to receive instructions on tightening the crank." (CPSC, "Huffy Recalls Bicycles Due to Cranks Falling Off; Riders Can Lose Control of Bike," October 16, 2007, Release #08-028.)

- Over 30,000 Triax PK7 and Vertical PK7 bikes, cheap kids' mountain bike–shaped objects, created by the Shun Lu Bicycle Company of Guangdong, China, and sold at Target stores, were recalled in 2007 after a few frames broke apart and injured the riders. Customers were offered a full refund at their nearest Target store. (CPSC, "Dynacraft Recalls Bicycles Sold Exclusively at Target Due to Frame Failure," March 28, 2007, Release #07-142.)

Below that price point, things rapidly get heavier and dumpier. There are some brands that will do the job for around $100. Check out the Vilano. At around this price, however, you may do well looking for a used bike of better quality.

FREE BIKES?

It happens. Thanks to the hard work put in by volunteers and the donations of Good Samaritans, several small organizations operate around the country that provide bicycles to low-income kids (and adults too) at little or no cost.

Free Bikes 4 Kidz, an organization serving the Twin Cities, has refurbished and gifted over 20,000 bikes since 2008, and is looking to expand. "The public donates gently used bikes, we organize thousands of volunteers to clean and refurbish them, and then we give them away to kids in need," is the group's simple stated purpose. ("Mission and Purpose," Free Bikes 4 Kidz website, fb4k .com/about/.) If you're in Minnesota, you can support this group with donations, time, money, and energy.

There is a catch here. If you're an individual in need of a bike, you can't get one directly from Free Bikes 4 Kidz. "Instead we only give our bikes away through a network of about 150 nonprofits, community organizations, churches, and schools in the Twin Cities metro area," explains the group's "Apply 4 Bikes" page.

Free Bikes 4 Kidz's major sponsor is Allina Health. Smaller groups operate that are more grassroots, but they tend to exist

Buying Used Kids' Bikes

Buying a used bike allows you to acquire a machine of much higher quality for the same price as a new mediocre or low-quality bike. Many are intimidated by the process, but learning to buy used really is an important and useful skill that will serve you well throughout your cycling life.

Of course, if cost is no issue, and you always buy new equipment, you can skip this section. But before you go, may we just say *Thank you* on behalf of the rest of us. You're the people who keep this process humming right along, by feeding barely used, high-quality bikes into the system. Thank you so much.

Now . . . before buying a used kids' bike, check the frame for cracks, bulges, bends, and other weirdness. Anything like that results in disqualification. Look at the bike from the side and make sure the fork is in line with the head tube and not bent back; if it is, that indicates the bike has experienced some sort of nasty head-on collision. (If only used bikes could talk.) Lean on a shoestring, and cease to exist rather suddenly. Many are full-service workshops where people can go and work on their own bikes with a full set of tools and knowledgeable mechanics available. Get involved with one of these places, donate some time, then take a free bike home to your grateful kid.

Here are some examples of rootsy nonprofits dedicated to helping people get on two wheels. Catch them while you can—or start your own!

Free Bikes 4 Kidz, Minneapolis-Saint Paul, fb4k.com/about/faq
Des Moines Bike Collective, Des Moines, dsmbikecollective.org
Kickstand Community Bike Shop, Knoxville, www.knoxbike
    collective.com.
Free Ride, Pittsburgh, freeridepgh.org.
The Recyclery Collective, Chicago, www.therecyclery.org.
Free Wheel Bicycle Workshop, Madison, freewheelbikes.org.
Bike Kitchen, San Francisco, bikekitchen.org.
The Bike Pit, Denver, bikepitdenver.com.
Mobo Bicycle Coop, Cincinnati, mobobicyclecoop.org.
Bike Oven, Los Angeles, bikeoven.com.

over and put some pressure on the handlebars, listening and feeling for anything out of the ordinary.

Spin the wheels. They should be true, or nearly so. Feel the spokes for tension. Loose spokes and wavy wheels are red flags, but may be easy to overcome if you've got some spoke wrench skills. Flat tires are annoying and certainly won't help the seller get rid of a kid's bike.

Check the brakes the way the CPSC does it, by standing over the bike and clamping the brake and rocking the bike back and forth. The brake should have enough power to hold the wheel, and the caliper should not move but remain fixed to the frame or fork. Do the same for the coaster brake, required on all American kids' bikes. If the bike only has a coaster brake, pay special attention to it.

A nasty-looking drivetrain might be easily resurrected and made like-new with a little bit of solvent and lubrication. (Note that solvent, like WD-40, and lubricant are not the same things. Don't spray solvent on a bike then fail to lubricate it.) If any drivetrain component is so worn that it needs to be replaced, however, it opens up a can of worms, and the bike most likely won't be worth your trouble.

If all goes well, you'll get your hot little hands on a bike that could honestly be described as barely used. Like new. There are many, many children's bikes out there that fit that description, sitting shunned and alone in sheds and garages across the country.

Product List

Diamondback Mini Viper. $160. Steel frame. 16-inch wheels. Coaster brake. Chain guard.

Early Rider Belter. $400. Aluminum frame. Belt drive. 16-inch wheels. Front and rear V-brakes (Internet sales only).

Islabikes Cnoc 14. $400. Aluminum frame. 14-inch wheels. Coaster brake and V-brake (US model).

Ridgeback MX14. £150. Aluminum frame. Also available in 12- and 16-inch sizes. V-brakes. *Note:* This is a UK company. Any "sidewalk bikes" sold in the United States must have a coaster brake. Chain case.

Spawn Cycles Furi. $385. Aluminum frame. 14-inch wheels. V-brakes. *Note:* This is a Canadian company. Any "sidewalk bikes" sold in the United States must have a coaster brake.

Specialized Hotrock. $240. Steel frame. 16-inch wheels (also available in 12-inch). Coaster brake. Chain guard.

Trek Mystic/Jet 16. $220. Steel frame. Coaster brake. Pads and chain case. (Mystic is the girls' model and Jet is the boys'.)

TykeBykes Pedal Bicycle. $189. Aluminum frame. 16-inch wheels. Coaster brake and front V-brake. Chain case and kickstand. No training wheels included.

Part Three:
KIDS ON BIKES

CHAPTER 16

Teaching Kids to Ride Safely

Some Scary Things

Kids are just naturally bad at traffic. Kids have a tougher time than adults processing the kind of information that needs to be processed to safely negotiate busy intersections. Putting them on bikes can send them over the edge. One way to think of it is that the mere act of riding the bike takes up more space in their brains, so they often don't have enough awareness left over to make good decisions around cars.

The normal child's general inability to process is sadly evident in crash and injury statistics. The proportion of children among injured cyclists is not as massive as it once was, but it's still very significant. Kids are still hugely overrepresented in crash statistics. Per hour of riding, kids are much more likely to be hurt than adults.

Children's injuries hold a commanding presence in the accident stats. Researchers almost never bother to separate the kids' stats from the adults', thus making normal adult cycling seem much more risky than it truly is. At the same time, bike-share systems around the country have shocked observers with their strikingly good safety records, largely because they provide

A huge percentage of collisions involving child bicyclists occur when the child rolls from a sidewalk or driveway into the street without looking. *curtis_creative/iStock/ Thinkstock* some of the only bicycling statistics without children's crashes. (Kids aren't allowed to use bike share.)

Kids are also much more likely to be the cause of any wreck they're involved in. While an adult cyclist is more than likely riding lawfully at the time of a wreck (believe it or not), kids are frighteningly prone to riding out of driveways and off sidewalks into the street, without looking, right in front of vehicles. And that's typically how kids are fatally injured while bicycling. For adults the pattern is strikingly different; the most common type of fatality involving an adult cyclist is a hit-from-behind collision on a high-speed road, through no fault of the rider involved.[1]

The pattern of carnage associated with child cycling suggests that something might be done to effectively minimize it. Something other than keeping kids off bikes. And that's about the only good news we can see when it comes to children's cycling injuries.

The Osmosis Theory

Teaching kids to ride bikes has become one of the easiest tasks in all of parenthood. Just put 'em on balance bikes and stand back. Teaching kids to ride safely, whether cruising their own neighborhoods, or back and forth to school, is more difficult, and scarier than ever.

Unfortunately, helmet wearing does not equate to traffic safety. We wish it were that simple. That said, make sure your kid wears a helmet whenever he rides. But you'll have to teach him about traffic safety as well, or the helmet could be pretty worthless.

Many parents say the process of teaching children to ride safely in cities and suburbs begins when the children are being hauled around by the parents. From seats on bikes or in cargo boxes the kids watch their parent's responses to various traffic situations, see their route choices in action, and begin to absorb the way of the street. Of course this works best if the routes and methods modeled are good ones.

In this osmosis theory of traffic learning, the most effective learning is said to take place if the child is actively pedaling along with the parent, shadowing them, or if the parent is cruising just behind and offering instructions. The latter can veer into "back seat driver" territory, highly annoying and repellent even to young kids, so watch out for that. By the time they're 9 or so, your kids are going to be highly sensitive to that stuff.

Between the getting-hauled stage and the riding stage, a child passes through a middle phase during which he can pedal a tandem or trail-a-bike with his parents. Parents report that this stage is very valuable for modeling traffic skills as well. Perhaps even more than when they're on their own bikes, kids pedaling as part of the same machines are shown, with no ambiguity, exactly where to line up in the traffic mix—if their parents are positioning themselves correctly. This kind of modeling can be really effective on a regular, daily route. If children see us doing the same thing over and over at an intersection, they will probably do the same thing themselves.

The Science of Learning about Traffic

Plenty of strong evidence exists in favor of the idea that kids might actually listen to what their parents are telling them, even about something as relatively tedious as traffic safety. They also watch and learn from what their parents are showing them.

Several studies support the idea that "individualized streetside training" makes a big difference for a kid's safety in traffic. Kids who ride with their parents understand the streets better than kids who don't.[2] It's a big, important head start.

Is it possible for kids to learn to ride safely by sitting in a class? From something easy like a video or Internet program, in front of which we can just plop them down for a while, like *Sesame Street*? A 2013 meta-study went looking for the answer to this question. Not really, the researchers concluded. Kids who took bike safety classes or some other form of passive training did not have better safety records after the training. They were no less likely to get hurt. Safety classes displayed some flashes of effectiveness in increasing knowledge of safe behavior, but when it came down to actually changing kids' behavior, the classes didn't seem to do a very good job.[3]

"Children trained using videos/software/Internet gained knowledge but did not change their behavior," wrote the authors of yet another study about teaching traffic safety to kids. In contrast, "Children trained individually gained in both knowledge and safer behavior."[4]

So teach your kids to ride safely as best you can, starting very early, long before they pedal their own bikes. Make every ride a learning experience. Show them how it's done. Then talk to them about what you're doing. Explain it all. If you can teach them not to ride blindly into the street, then half the battle is won.

Teach them the rules, but also teach them defensive cycling. Teach them not to assume that drivers or pedestrians will notice them. Teach them to ride patiently and with vigilance. Talk to them about, and demonstrate, how to properly handle the machine—things like looking through turns and body control under hard braking.

You can see what this is all coming down to. There is no balance bike for learning traffic safety. The key to your child's safety while bicycling is you.

How Young Is Too Young?

How young is too young to, say, ride to school or a friend's house? To go off on one's own for the first time? There isn't much hard science to dictate to parents how old their kids should be before riding alone. But one number comes up again and again when we ask this question. Nine. Nine years old. Why 9? It has to do with the stages of kids' development, and conventional wisdom, derived from the actual experiences of parents and kids around the world. Nine is usually when it happens. Eight to 10, somewhere in there.

As in other aspects of family biking, parents need to take this age guideline with a grain of salt. It's not as if a kid wakes up on his ninth birthday with traffic knowledge installed. The child's readiness isn't based on his age, but on his experience so far, and the things you taught him while you were riding and walking together. The child may not be ready at any age. The child may not be ready at 40. One thing is pretty certain: The kid will want to go off on her own before she is ready to do so safely.

John Forester, the godfather of "vehicular cycling," thinks that kids can learn to ride safely in traffic at age 9 simply by following the vehicular rules of the road. Forester's idea is simple and easy, and is based on an assumption that drivers are near-perfect in their attention and rule-following. If such a world existed, then a 9-year-old wouldn't have much trouble bicycling through it.

On the other hand, our long experience has showed us that traffic is an environment defined by human mistakes, not near perfection. If this better describes the reality of traffic, and we think it does, then simply following vehicular rules is an inadequate safety strategy—for children and adults alike. Anybody on the streets needs to be ever ready to counter the sort of driver fails that ultimately define the experience of being there.

Unfortunately, statistics confirm that those who bike according to the laws, even if they make zero mistakes, are still vulnerable to the mistakes of others. So something more is required of bicyclists in this world. A certain frostiness. Vigilance, and anticipation. The proverbial "eyes in the back of your head." A lot of patience. These things are pretty rare to find in a 9-year-old.

We're not saying you should keep your 9-year-old off the bike and off the streets. But before setting the kid loose on urban streets or high-speed roads, make sure she knows and follows the rules, and understands very well how vulnerable she remains to being overlooked while doing so.

CHAPTER 17

The Future of Kids' Bicycling

The Big Change

Over the past forty years, the United States has undergone a frightening transformation. We're not talking about the cancer-like spread of soulless strip malls and suburbs across the prairies. We're not talking about the rise of extremist politics or the shocking decline in public discourse. No, we're talking about a transformation that has barely been noticed or spoken of. But, make no mistake, it is huge. It has already changed this country in ways we can only begin to imagine.

We're talking about the decline—you could almost call it a disappearance—of child cycling in this country.

When we were kids, we rode bikes. A lot. So did all of our friends. And that's pretty much the way it was across the nation. You didn't have to be a bike lover or enthusiast of any sort to ride a bike, it was just something that American kids did. Those of you who were born after, say, 1980, may not fully grasp just how inseparable kids' bicycling was from American suburban culture. Check out the blockbuster *E.T.* for a view of suburbia during the time when childhood and bicycling were intimately related. At some point, and nobody knows exactly why, this started to change in a big way.

After decades of decline in child cycling, where do we go from here?
gbh007/iStock/Thinkstock

Although The Big Change has never been addressed head on by government agencies or academia, we can see it reflected strikingly in bicycling statistics of various types. An obvious one is the percentage of kids who ride bikes to school. It's dwindled to a tiny percentage. It wasn't always so small. We also see it in crash statistics. In the 1970s bicycling was so popular with American kids that the vast majority of cyclist crashes involved kids under 16. These days the kids' share of crashes is far lower. In a sense that's good news—children's bicycling injuries and fatalities have dropped precipitously—but it's not because of safety interventions, it's primarily because kids don't ride bikes nearly as much, or in the same way as they did. The culture has changed. It would be very difficult to argue that it has changed for the better with regard to kids on bikes.

Certainly this change has not raised many alarms among those who should have noticed it. Bicycling advocates rarely mention it, and their campaigns almost never address it. Who wants to be seen as calling for more injured or killed kids? Government officials charged with overseeing the health and welfare of children don't decry the decline in child cycling. In fact, they almost seem to welcome it. It makes us wonder. Was the decline in child cycling all part of the Plan?

Helmet laws might have had something to do with the decline, although it's hard to pin down exactly how much effect they had. Many point to mandatory helmet legislation as the primary culprit. Others say that the helmet laws are just part of an overarching cultural shift that has transformed the lives of children—the safety cult. Even with helmets, parents are less likely to let kids ride.

Let's not forget that bicycling—while potentially dangerous—is very healthy exercise, and a form of clean transportation to boot, which should be promoted instead of discouraged. Let's do what we can to promote a new Big Change, in the opposite direction.

Pedal Forward

Many of us dream of a world in which kids can ride safely without having to be drilled in defensive cycling by their paranoid parents. We think of schools in Copenhagen and Amsterdam, where the vast majority of kids arrive by bike—their own bikes or on board their parents'. There is no screeching of tires or rumbling of diesel bus engines, no parents road-raging at each other, just the sound of happy children and bike chains whirring. It seems almost mythical to us, but these places are real. We wonder, naturally, what makes that possible there when it seems so impossible here.

Infrastructure is the simplest answer. Everyone knows about all those cycle tracks that make biking easy and comfortable. Bicycling parents in the United States demand them, and understandably so, but is that all there is to it? If it were possible to get all the cycle tracks, would that be enough? Will that unleash the American bike renaissance?

When you really examine what happened in Europe, infrastructure turns out to be just part of the picture. Bicycling in the Netherlands and Denmark benefits from a number of policies and realities that are unknown to North America. For example, much lower speed limits on urban streets. And the laws—the rules of engagement for bikes and cars—are fundamentally different, skewed toward bicyclists and other vulnerable road users. Imagine that!

Finally, the biggest reason for such high levels of cycling in Northern Europe could be the price of fuel, which those governments deliberately keep at astronomical levels compared to what we're used to in the United States. How much more likely would people be to ride a bike if gas were around $7 a gallon? How much more likely would they be to support bike lanes and other changes to make bicycling better and easier? How much easier would it be to pay for these things?[1]

With American activists currently so focused on cycle tracks and protected bike lanes, a lot of the other good stuff is being neglected—things like off-street paths in their own rights-of-way, which function like freeways for bikes, passing beneath all streets and intersections. Things like woonerfs, streets where drivers must drive extremely slowly and defer to all other road users, opposite of the usual arrangement. Things like low speed limits and bike-friendly laws. Even, dare we imagine, a realistic gas tax.

It's possible that we could get that network of bike lanes, and yet still end up further from the ideal than we were before, as the world outside the lines goes ever more to the dark side. And that won't make it any easier for your kid to ride around his neighborhood or get to school under his own power. Let's take a more holistic approach to rebuilding a culture of bicycling for kids in the United States.

Learn about the following organizations that are committed to getting kids on bikes and making better riding environments for everyone:

Safe Routes to School. Over the decades the number of kids who ride bikes to school has plummeted. That's really saying something, because in the United States the number was never all that high to begin with. Now school zones are some of the most traffic-intensive places in the country, dangerous and scary places for little pedestrians and bicyclists to be. The worse they became, the less likely parents were to let their kids commute to school on foot or bike, so the situation just got worse and worse. That's absurd, and we need to reverse that cycle. Research shows the Safe Routes to School Program is somewhat effective in increasing the proportion of kids who commute to school under their own power.[2]

Kidical Mass. You might hate Critical Mass, but you gotta love Kidical Mass. This isn't a very formal group, but there are a number of active chapters in communities around the country, promoting the general idea of kids on bikes in America. Their gatherings of wheeled families are some of the most effective traffic calming measures imaginable. They get people used to seeing kids and families on the streets, and they're fun too. If there isn't a chapter in your city, maybe you should start one!

People for Bikes. Formerly Bikes Belong, People for Bikes is a power coalition of industry and community bike lobbyists, working to shape policy in their favor. Bend their ear to let them know you care about the holistic approach mentioned above.

Notes

Chapter 1

1. "ACOG Committee Opinion: Exercise During Pregnancy and the Postpartum period," *International Journal of Gynecology and Obstetrics* 77, 2002, pp. 79–81.

2. Diane Duncombe, Virginia Fraser, Leanne Kelly, Susan J. Paxton, Helen Skouteris, and Eleanor H. Wertheim, "Vigorous exercise and birth outcomes in a sample of recreational exercisers: A prospective study across pregnancy," *Australian and New Zealand Journal of Obstetrics and Gynaecology* 46, 2006, pp. 288–92.

3. "Perceived Exertion," CDC website, last updated March 20, 2011, accessed October 20, 2014, www.cdc.gov/physicalactivity/everyone/measuring/exertion.html.

4. R. Artal and M. O'Toole, "Guidelines of the American College of Obstetricians and Gynecologists for exercise during pregnancy and the postpartum period," *British Journal of Sports Medicine*, Vol. 37, 2003.

5. "ACOG Committee Opinion," p. 79.

6. Zewditu Demissie, Nancy Dole, Kelly R. Evenson, Bradley N. Gaynes, Amy Herring, and Anna Maria Siega-Riz, "Physical activity and depressive symptoms among pregnant women: the PIN3 study," *Archives of Women's Health*, April 2011, pp. 145–57.

7. Timothy J. Bungum, Allen W. Jackson, Dian L. Peaslee, and Miguel A. Perez, "Exercise During Pregnancy and Type of Delivery in Nulliparae," *Journal of Obstetric, Gynecologic & Neonatal Nursing*, May 2000, pp. 258–64.

8. Michel Boulvain, Bengt Kayser, and Katarina Melzer, "Physical activity and pregnancy: Cardiovascular Adaptations, Recommendations and Pregnancy Outcomes," *Sports Medicine*, Vol. 40, No. 6, 2010, pp. 493–507.

9. See Faith Brynie, "Exercise During Pregnancy Aids Infant's Brain Development," *Psychology Today*, November 12, 2013. https://www.psychologytoday.com/blog/brain-sense/201311/exercise-during-pregnancy-aids-infants-brain-development

10. E-mail correspondence with Alexis Rohde.

11. "ACOG Committee Opinion," p. 80.

12. Artal and O'Toole, "Guidelines of the American College of Obstetricians and Gynecologists."

13. Amit Bhattacharya, Kari Dunning, and Grace LeMasters, "A Major Public Health Issue: The High Incidence of Falls During Pregnancy," *Maternal and Child Health Journal*, 2010, pp. 720–25.

14. E-mail correspondence with Alexis Rohde.

15. "The 13 Rules of Safe Pregnancy Exercise," Baby Center, accessed October 21, 2014, www.babycenter.com/0_the-13-rules-of-safe-pregnancy-exercise_622.bc.

16. E-mail correspondence with Danielle Givens.

17. Haruna, Matsuzaki, Murayama, Ota, Shiraishi, Watanabe, Yeo, and Yoshida, "The effects of an exercise program on health-related quality of life in postpartum mothers: A randomized controlled trial." *Health*, 2013, pp. 432–39. www.scirp.org/journal/PaperInformation.aspx?PaperID=28696#.VZQ4j0ahtAM

18. Sioban L. Kane, "Does Exercise Alleviate the Symptoms of Postpartum Depression?" PCOM Physician Assistant Studies Student Scholarship, Paper 70, 2012.

19. E-mail correspondence with Alexis Rohde.

Chapter 2

1. E-mail correspondence with Jonathan Maus.

2. Patricia Kennett, ed., *A Handbook of Comparative Social Policy*, 2nd ed. Edward Elgar Publishing, 2013, p. 315. Bruno Martorano, Luisa Natali, Chris de Neubourg, and Jonathan Bradshaw, "Child Well-Being in Advanced Economies in the Late 2000s," *Social Indicators Research*, Vol. 118, No. 1, August 2014, pp. 247–83. Abstract: http://link.springer.com/article/10.1007/s11205-013-0402-z.

3. See Frieda Hulka and Joseph Piatt, "An Infant in a Car Seat on a Washing Machine: Epidural Hematoma," *Pediatrics*, Vol. 94, No. 4, October 1, 1994, pp. 556–57. This paper highlights the case of a 7-month-old baby who was put in a car seat and placed on a washing machine in hopes the vibration would calm him. It's a fairly common practice. In this case the car seat fell off the machine and the child suffered a serious head injury and nearly died. Falls while strapped into a car seat can be especially dangerous, because the baby can't right itself while strapped in, and because of the extra mass of the seat. This is something to think about if you are a parent who carries your kid in a car seat in a *bakfiets*. Strapping the seat securely to the cargo box should be enough to keep your child safe from a disastrous car seat–enhanced head injury in the event of a crash. Be absolutely certain that the cargo box is well secured to the bike as well.

Chapter 3

1. Amit Gupta, *Industrial Safety and Environment*, Firewall Media, 2006, p. 155. Massimo Bovenzi, "Health Disorders Caused by Occupational Exposure to Vibration," in Francesco Violante, Asa Kilborn, and T. J. Armstrong, *Occupational Ergonomics: Work Related Musculoskeletal Disorders of the Upper Limb and Back*, CRC Press, 2000, pp. 89–94.

2. Quoted in Marion Rice, "Carrying your infant by bike: How young is too young?" bikeportland.org, August 24, 2009, http://bikeportland .org/2009/08/24/carrying-your-infant-by-bike-how-young-is-too-young -22374.

3. Laura Levine and Joyce Munsch, *Child Development: An Active Learning Approach*, SAGE, 2010, p. 195.

4. Sean Deoni, Doublas Dean, Jonathan O'Muircheartaigh, Holly Dirks, and Beth Jerskey, "Investigating white matter development in infancy and early childhood using myelin water faction and relaxation time mapping," *NeuroImage*, Vol. 63, 2012, pp. 1038–53.

5. J. Giacomin and S. Gallo, "In-vehicle vibration study of child safety seats," *Ergonomics*, Vol. 46, No. 15, 2003, pp. 1500–12. The authors of this study, noting that "few studies have been performed regarding the vibrational stimuli reaching the child occupant," measured levels of vibration transmitted to adult drivers as well as children in car seats, using accelerometers. Surprisingly, they found that "the system composed of automobile seat, child seat and child was found to transmit greater vibration than the system composed of automobile seat and driver." Park, Min, Subramaniyam, and Lee, et al., "Vibration Effect Investigation in Baby Car Seats and Automobile Seats," SAE Technical Paper 2014-01-0462, 2014. Malin Nilsson, "Health risk aspects and comfort for infants in infant seats for cars," Master's Thesis, University of Linkoping, 2005, www.diva-portal.org/smash/get/diva2:670258/FULLTEXT01.pdf.

6. American Academy of Pediatrics, Committee on Injury and Poison Prevention, "Bicycle Helmets," *Pediatrics*, Vol. 108, No. 4, October 1, 2001, pp. 1030–32, http://pediatrics.aappublications.org/content/108/4/1030. full?sid=e5a68282-0b58-46e0-9254-82f4ff773c8c. The recommendation was reaffirmed in late 2011.

7. Amy Paller, John Hawk, Paul Honig, Yoke Chin Giam, Steven Hoath, Catherine Mack, and Georgios Stamatas, "New Insights About Infant and Toddler Skin: Implications for Sun Protection," *Pediatrics*, Vol. 128, No. 1, July 1, 2011, pp. 92–102.

8. US Food and Drug Administration, "Should You Put Sunscreen on Infants? Not Usually," May 6, 2014, www.fda.gov/ForConsumers/ConsumerUpdates/ ucm309136.htm.

9. Sonya Lunder, "Pick the Best Sunscreen For Kids," Environmental Working Group's Enviroblog, July 4, 2012, www.ewg.org/enviroblog/2012/07/pick-best-sunscreen-kids.

10. "Get the best sunscreen for babies and kids," *Consumer Reports*, May 2012, www.consumerreports.org/cro/2012/05/get-the-best-sunscreen-for-babies-and-kids/index.htm.

11. US Food and Drug Administration, "FDA Sheds Light on Sunscreens," May 17, 2012, www.fda.gov/ForConsumers/ConsumerUpdates/ucm258416.htm.

12. E. Ernst and M. H. Pittler, "Efficacy of ginger for nausea and vomiting: a systemic review of randomized clinical trials," *British Journal of Anaesthesia*, Vol. 84, 2000, pp. 367–71. This meta-study of clinical trials involving ginger suggests that the root can relieve motion sickness and some other types of nausea.

13. National Electronic Injury Surveillance System (NEISS), www.cpsc.gov/en/Research--Statistics/NEISS-Injury-Data/.

14. The National Electronic Injury Surveillance System estimates a half million ER visitors each year and another half million outpatients. If we accept that many cyclists crash and suffer minor injuries but don't seek medical attention, then there are "millions" of injuries. Just how many millions is not known.

15. Web-based Injury Statistics Query and Reporting System (WISQARS), www.cdc.gov/injury/wisqars/.

16. Petula Dvorak, "Why I let my kids walk to the corner store—and why other parents should, too," *Washington Post*, August 25, 2014.

Chapter 5

1. Connecticut Revised Statutes. Title 14, Chapter 248, Sec. 14-286d, www.cga.ct.gov/current/pub/chap_248.htm#sec_14-286d.

2. CPSC, "Safety Standard for Bicycle Helmets; Final Rule," 16 CFR Part 1203, Federal Register, Vol. 63, No. 46, March 10, 1998, www.cpsc.gov//PageFiles/86318/10mr98r.pdf.

3. Frederick P. Rivara, MD, MPH, Diane C. Thompson, MS, and Robert S. Thompson, MD, "Circumstances and Severity of Bicycle Injuries," Snell Memorial Foundation/Harborview Injury Prevention and Research Center (1996).

4. Robert S. Thompson, MD, Frederick P. Rivara, MD, MPH, and Diane C. Thompson, MS, "A Case Control Study of the Effectiveness of Bicycle Safety Helmets," *The New England Journal of Medicine*, May 1989, pp. 1361–67.

5. Diane C. Thompson, MS, Frederick P. Rivara, MD, MPH, and Robert S. Thompson, MD, "Effectiveness of Bicycle Safety Helmets in Preventing Head

Injuries," *Journal of the American Medical Association*, December 1996, pp. 1968–73.

6. Letter from Jim Sundahl to US Consumer Product Safety Commission, January 20, 1998, www.cpsc.gov//PageFiles/79325/34c7a89b.pdf.

7. Patrick Bishop, Blaine Hoshizaki, Marshall Kendall, and Andrew Post, "Performance Criteria for a Child-Specific Helmet," ASTM International, June 2014. Abstract: www.astm.org/DIGITAL_LIBRARY/STP/PAGES/STP155220120145.htm.

8. www.cpsc.gov/en/Safety-Education/Safety-Guides/Sports-Fitness -and-Recreation/Bicycles/Which-Helmet-for-Which-Activity/.

9. For instance see "Heads Up: Concussion Fact Sheet For Parents," Center for Disease Control, www.cdc.gov/headsup/pdfs/custom/headsupconcussion _fact_sheet_for_parents.pdf.

10. "CPSC Issues New Safety Standard for Bike Helmets," Release #98062, www .cpsc.gov/en/Newsroom/News-Releases/1998/CPSC-Issues-New-Safety -Standard-for-Bike-Helmets/.

11. CPSC recall notices, www.cpsc.gov. These reports detail the approximate number of recalled helmets that were sold, and the reasons for their recall. (See the "Youth Helmet Recalls" sidebar on page 56.)

Chapter 6

1. "Bike trailer buying guide," consumerreports.org, www.consumerreports.org/ cro/bike-trailers/buying-guide.htm.

Chapter 7

1. Robert Tanz and Katherine Christoffel, "Tykes on Bikes: Injuries associated with bicycle-mounted child seats," Pediatric Emergency Care, October 1991. This report looked at Consumer Product Safety Commission data from 1978 to 1988.

2. Elizabeth Powell and Robert Tanz, "Tykes and Bikes: Injuries Associated With Bicycle-Towed Child Trailers and Bicycle-Mounted Child Seats," 1999, http:// archpedi.jamanetwork.com/article.aspx?articleid=348997#ArticleInformation.

3. Ashley Zeilinski, Lynne Rochette, and Gary Smith, "Stair-Related Injuries to Young Children Treated in U.S. Emergency Departments, 1999-2008," *Pediatrics*, Vol. 129, No. 4, April 1, 2012, pp. 721–27.

4. Shinya Miyamoto and Shigenori Inoue, "Reality and risk of contact-type head injuries related to bicycle-mounted child seats," *Journal of Safety Research*, December 2010, pp. 501–5.

Chapter 8

1. American Academy of Pediatrics, "The Child As Passenger On An Adult's Bicycle," The Injury Prevention Program (TIPP) handout, 1994.

2. E-mail correspondence with Jonathan Maus.

3. "Bike trailer buying guide," consumerreports.org, www.consumerreports.org/cro/bike-trailers/buying-guide.htm.

4. Mark Widome, ed., *Injury Prevention and Control for Children and Youth*, American Academy of Pediatrics, 1997, p. 347.

5. Trisha Korioth, "Pedal safely when biking with baby on board," *AAP News*, 2009, accessed September 6, 2014, http://aapnews.aappublications.org/content/30/7/18.6.full.

6. American Academy of Pediatrics, "The Child As Passenger On An Adult's Bicycle." This guidance was reprinted in "Baby On Board: Keeping Safe on a Bike," healthychildren.org (American Academy of Pediatrics), updated June 13, 2014, www.healthychildren.org/English/safety-prevention/at-play/Pages/Baby-On-Board-Keeping-Safe-On-A-Bike.aspx.

7. Elizabeth Powell and Robert Tanz, "Tykes and Bikes: Injuries Associated With Bicycle-Towed Child Trailers and Bicycle-Mounted Child Seats." 1999, http://archpedi.jamanetwork.com/article.aspx?articleid=348997#ArticleInformation.

Chapter 9

1. Eric McKeegan, "Bike Review: Gazelle Cabby," Bicycle Times, August 6, 2013, http://bicycletimesmag.com/review-gazelle-cabby/. McKeegan writes, "I've noticed a lot of Dutch bikes are not equipped with powerful brakes, which is O.K. for flatter areas."

2. Quoted from Joe Bike website, www.joe-bike.com/bikes/the-shuttlebug-handmade-in-portland/.

3. Post on mtbr.com forums, in thread "Quest for a Bakfiets: Virtue Bikes Schoolbus and Gondoliere," January 19, 2014, http://forums.mtbr.com/cargo-bikes/quest-bakfiets-virtue-bikes-schoolbus-gondoliere-892832.html.

4. Quoted from Winther website, www.wintherbikes.com/en/product/wallaroo#quicktabs-producttabs=6.

Chapter 10

1. E-mail correspondence with Patrick Barber.

2. Price from J.C. Lind Bike Company website, Chicago, 2014. http://www.jclindbikes.com/bikes/kangaroo.

Chapter 11

1. US Consumer Product Safety Commission, "Yuba Bicycles Recalls Mundo Cargo Bikes Due to Injury Hazard," March 20, 2013, Recall number 13-144.

2. "We tried it: Surly Big Dummy (with and without BionX electric assist)," Hum of the City (blog), September 17, 2012, http://humofthecity.com/2012/09/17/we-tried-it-surly-big-dummy-with-and-without-bionx-electric-assist/.

3. "Xtracycle reinvents its own with EdgeRunner, and some backstory," clevercycles.com, October 30, 2012, https://clevercycles.com/blog/2012/10/30/xtracycle-reinvents-its-own-with-edgerunner-and-some-backstory/.

4. "We tried it: Xtracycle EdgeRunner (prototype)," Hum of the City (blog), December 14, 2012, http://humofthecity.com/2012/12/14/we-tried-it-xtracycle-edgerunner/.

Chapter 12

1. Tony Hadland and Hans-Erhard Lessing, *Bicycle Design: An Illustrated History* (Cambridge: The MIT Press, 2014), p. 377.

Chapter 13

1. Price from the website of Clever Cycles, Portland, Oregon, 2014, http://clevercycles.com/kidztandem-family-bike-latte.

2. Price from Co-Motion website, http://co-motion.com/index.php/bikes/periscope-scout.

3. Price from the website of Wheel House Bikes in Santa Barbara, California, 2014, www.wheelhousebikes.com/product_details.cfm?id=140&catid=78. *Note:* This bike shop includes the second seat as standard equipment. If you order elsewhere, you might have to pay extra for the second saddle and footrest package.

4. Price from Workcycles website, 2014, www.workcycles.com/home-products/child-transport-bicycles/onderwater-family-tandem-xl.

Chapter 14

1. Website of Miir company. www.miir.com/product_p/500226-500229.htm. See also Ali Browning, "Give Back With Miir Bikes," Seattle Magazine, April 2013, www.seattlemag.com/article/give-back-miir-bikes; and Rachel Lerman, "Beer, coffee and shopping: Miir tries a new retail concept in Brooks Sports building," *Puget Sound Business Journal*, September 5, 2014, www.bizjournals.com/seattle/blog/2014/09/beer-coffee-and-shopping-miir-tries-a-new-retail.html?page=all.

2. www.kidsbalancebikes.com/all-balance-bikes/firstbike-composite-bikes/.

3. According to a review of the bike on Two Wheeling Tots from 2013: www
   .twowheelingtots.com/specialized/.

Chapter 15

1. The CPSC's guidance for businesses states: "Bicycles must have front and rear
   brakes, or rear brakes only. Sidewalk bikes may not have hand brakes only.
   Sidewalk bikes with a seat height of 22 inches or more when adjusted in the
   lowest position must have a foot brake. A sidewalk bike with a seat height
   of less than 22 inches need not have any brake as long as it does not have a
   freewheeling feature, has a permanent label saying 'No brakes,' and has the
   same statement on its advertising and shipping cartons." A "sidewalk bicycle" is
   defined as a bicycle with a seat that is no higher than 25 inches off the ground
   when placed at the highest position, which covers almost all 14- and 16-inch
   bicycles. US Consumer Product Safety Commission, "Bicycle Requirements
   Business Guidance," August 1, 2002, www.cpsc.gov/Business--Manufacturing/
   Business-Education/Business-Guidance/Bicycle-Requirements/.

2. Brian Holcombe, "Review: Islabikes Cnoc delivers aggressive, durable ride
   for kids," *VeloNews*, May 9, 2014, http://velonews.competitor.com/2014/05/
   bikes-and-tech/reviews/review-islabikes-cnoc-delivers-aggressive-durable-ride
   -kids_326905.

3. Furi description, Spawn Cycles website, http://spawncycles.com/shop/
   spawn-cycles-furi/.

Chapter 16

1. Ken McLeod and Liz Murphy, "Every Bicyclist Counts." League of American
   Bicyclists, May, 2014.

2. David Schwebel, Leslie McClure, and Joan Seveson, "Teaching children to cross
   streets safely: A randomized, controlled trial," *Health Psychology*, July 2014,
   pp. 628–38. Abstract: http://psycnet.apa.org/psycinfo/2014-01826-001/.
   Ugo Lachapelle, Robert Noland, and Leigh Ann Von Hagen, "Teaching
   children about bicycle safety: An evaluation of the New Jersey Bike School
   program," *Accident Analysis & Prevention*, March 28, 2013, p. 1. This study of the
   effectiveness of a kids' bike safety program in New Jersey found that "children
   who bicycled with their parents scored higher on the pre-training test but
   did not improve as much on the post-training test." Benjamin Baron, David
   Schwebel, and Barara A. Morrongiello, "Brief Report: Increasing Children's
   Safe Pedestrian Behaviors through Simple Skills Training," *Journal of Pediatric
   Psychology*, Vol. 32, No. 4, 2007, pp. 475–80, http://jpepsy.oxfordjournals.org/
   content/32/4/475.full.

3. Sarah Richmond, Yu Janice Zhang, Andi Stover, Andrew Howard, and
   Colin Macarthur, "Prevention of bicycle-related injuries in children and

youth: a systemic review of bicycle skills training interventions," *Injury Prevention*, November 21, 2013, http://injuryprevention.bmj.com/content/early/2013/11/21/injuryprev-2013-040933.full.

4. David Schwebel and Leslie McClure, "Training Children in Pedestrian Safety: Distinguishing Gains in Knowledge from Gains in Safe Behavior," *The Journal of Primary Prevention*, February 27, 2014, p. 151, http://link.springer.com/article/10.1007/s10935-014-0341-8#page-1.

Chapter 17

1. The majority of Americans become snarly when faced with a hint of a suggestion that taxes should be raised; they become triple snarly about any suggestion that taxes should be raised to fund cycling infrastructure. A common argument related to this holds that bicyclists should pay "road taxes" and registration fees like drivers, especially when it comes to funding bike-only projects. Most of those who make this argument don't realize that bicyclists already pay "road taxes," as the funds for local roads come primarily from local sales and property taxes. Because bicyclists don't impart wear and tear on the roads like drivers of motor vehicles, but pay plenty of local taxes, bicyclists are actually subsidizing the motorists on local roads. Bicycling doesn't automatically add to the Highway Trust Fund, as driving does through fuel taxes, but bicyclists aren't allowed to ride on highways, for the most part. Fuel taxes pay for a smaller and smaller chunk of the highway system's construction and maintenance, so the shortfall is made up from the general fund, paid by all taxpayers, bicyclists included. It's true that even non-drivers benefit in some ways from the highway system. It's more difficult to get non-cyclists to understand that they benefit from a well-designed system of bikeways.

2. Noreen McDonald, Ruth Steiner, Chanam Lee, Tori Rhoulac Smith, Xuemel Zhu, and Yizhao Yang, "Impact of the Safe Routes to School Program on Walking and Bicycling," *Journal of the American Planning Association*, Vol. 80, No. 2, September 25, 2014, pp. 153–67.

About the Authors

Robert Hurst is an ex-messenger, amateur historian, and stay-at-home dad. He is also the author of *The Art of Cycling, The Cyclist's Manifesto, The Art of Mountain Biking: Singletrack Skills for All Riders, Best Bike Rides Denver and Boulder, Mountain Biking Colorado's San Juan Mountains, Road Biking Colorado,* and *Road Biking Colorado's Front Range* (FalconGuides).

Christie Hurst is an ex-messenger and veteran special education teacher who commutes across the city and back almost every day. When not riding bikes or mothering, she retires to her mountain redoubt and hatches plots.